AUTHENTIC FAITH:

Feeding the Soul in Politically Divided Times

Authentic Faith:

Feeding the Soul in Politically Divided Times

Encouragement for
Jesus Followers,
Justice Seekers,
Resisters,
Immigrant Supporters,
and
Peacemakers

Mike Rumley-Wells

Rumley-Wells, Mike

ISBN: 978-0-578-78119-8

For Kim
always

Contents

Introduction

1 Grace Frees Us to Try

2 I Don't Want to Hate

3 Love your enemies and pray for those who persecute you

4 We've all lost friends

5 Name-calling

6 Exhaustion

7 I Need You to Admit You're Wrong

8 Matthew 25 and Loving Jesus

9 A Horrible Day in the Neighborhood

10 When a Life Matters

11 Being Right Versus Being Loving

12 The Argument for Arguing

13 Intellectual Dishonesty

14 Repentance

15 Grieving Our Broken *Shalom*

16 Kindness Is More

17 Monday Grace

18 Tuesday Grace

19 Wednesday Grace

20 Thursday Grace

21 Friday Grace

22 Saturday Grace

23 Sunday Grace

24 Culture Shock, Grief, and Pandemic

25 Believing the Best, Optimism, and Wishful Thinking

26 Cheery? Civil? Gracious.

27 Lament

28 Cynicism versus Hope

29 Light in the Darkness

30 Hope

31 Malaise

32 Mirth

33 I Still Believe

34 Gaslighting

35 Regarding Others in Light of What They've Suffered

36 Help Them as a Priest

37 What Matters

Epilogue I: My Thoughts on Kids in Cages

Epilogue II: A Few More Thoughts on Life, Death, RHE, and
        Where I Go from Here

Introduction

Help me, Jesus.

I want to live this faith. I want to take Jesus seriously and integrate his words and actions into my life. I want to depend on God's spirit to give me strength and peace and a better sense of humor.

I want to love people. I want to love people better and *more*. I want to love my neighbor as myself. I want to love myself.

I want to live by grace. I want to embrace grace for myself and offer grace to others. I want to learn how to show grace *and* speak truth, both at once. Jesus did both, all the time, even when he spoke hard truth that his listeners didn't want to hear. Jesus did not treat truth and grace as mutually exclusive.

For a long time—for most of my life—I apologized for many of the things I say. I kept thinking that if people disagreed with me, or got upset at what I said, I *must* be doing something wrong.

Jesus doesn't actually say that.

For years, I believed, deep down, that I *should* be able to convince people and, if I couldn't, that meant I was failing.

Jesus didn't say that, either.

I'm not writing this against anyone. I'm writing this *for* you, to encourage you. But some people will not like what I've written. I'm speaking up because enough people have let me know that hearing my voice helps them and we need all the encouragement and hope we can muster right now. I'm slow and thick-headed and wildly, irrationally insecure, plus I desperately want everyone to like, approve of, respect, and praise me. I'm confessing those things and repenting of them. I manifest my repentance by writing and speaking up as faithfully as I know how and leaving the judgment to God.

If my title speaks to you, you know why I've written this book. We're overwhelmed by evidence about what's wrong. Our picture of *shalom* contrasts sharply with what we see happening now and we feel compelled to work toward justice in all of this. I'm offering encouragement, not evidence. If you believe this administration have done everything well, are a Christian's "dream" administration, and that *I*, questioning their behavior as I do, am the real problem, you probably won't like this book. I do realize many of these objections can go both ways. I'd still love to have you read it, if only to try to understand better. But if you know in your soul the *shalom* we seek, a love that unites and casts out all fear instead of...this, then you know we can't keep silent.

"Authentic" is not a boast. "Authentic" means "real" or "genuine." It doesn't mean "perfect," "better," or "to a higher standard." I'm not suggesting that this is the only way to live an authentic faith—heck, I'm not even trying to tell you how to live an authentic faith, only to encourage you to continue living your faith that *is* authentic. I'm also not suggesting that others' faith is inauthentic. That's between them and God, not me and them nor me and God. When I was a young new Christian, I wanted to live a "radical" faith. Now I understand that any belief in Jesus I can live will be radical. I don't need to make it radical; I need only to follow Jesus. Offering love and grace in this storm of hatred and fear? God's *shalom* and justice *are* radical.

I am speaking up. I am not the only one saying these things but I *am* saying them. I've felt horribly discouraged by what I'm seeing some other Christians do and say in the past four years. I understand that sounds judgmental. But I'm not repenting of saying it. If we can't speak against wrong *while* offering grace, then we have either lost sight of Jesus or misunderstood grace.

We also have to accept that we won't solve everything with a different President. We have seen symptoms, not the cause. We have so much work to do even when we have put this part behind us. It's pleasant to imagine that a change of administration will let us "go back to normal." But "normal" got us here. If we seek justice and *shalom*—if we seek God's Kingdom—we need to feed our souls for a much longer journey.

While sitting in church, I suddenly got the idea to write this book of reflections as a response to a friend's encouragement. Here's the context. I wrote in a blog post:

The most difficult part, for me, of being a Christian is other Christians. I will say that straight out. If I'm honest, I then have to ask if I am the most difficult part of being a Christian for some other people. I might be. Sometimes I don't believe what they believe or speak like they speak.

My friend responded:
Considering the above quote, I would mull over the converse as well. For some, the only thing keeping them from going full-blown, angry anti-theist...is a solitary individual within the tradition of Jesus who is doing their best to live a faith that is authentic without being logic-phobic or politically compromised. I'm not even going to pretend I'm not writing about you.

Jesus saves and redeems and loves us. He also confronts and corrects us. I do not quote my friend as a boast. "He is the source of your life in Christ Jesus, who became for us wisdom from God, and righteousness and sanctification and redemption, in order that, as it is written, 'Let the one who boasts, boast in the Lord.'" (I Corinthians 1:30-31) Okay, I also boast in my wife. I'm not claiming credit for anything other than what God does through me, which is a gift and not my own strength. But giving someone hope is a big deal. I cried when I read what my friend wrote. If I can encourage more people this way, I'm going to try.

If you aren't a Jesus follower, *thank you* for making the effort both to read this and to translate it into your own terminology. I try to avoid lingo but I write from my perspective and experience. Living in Nicaragua drove home for me that how I see the world is *not* the only, nor the objective, perception. I fervently hope I write to include, not exclude. If anything here resonates as truth to you, then I am encouraged. By all means, let me know!

The saying goes, "Write the book you need that no one else has written." I'm trying. I'm trying to write the book that I would need—that I *do* need—to help me keep going. I cannot begin to express how exhausting I find our present time. I hear the same from my friends. I hope this book becomes dated so that readers look at it years from now and can't relate to living in the days we are living through right now. We have a long way to go to get there.

Enough explanation. I'm talking to you now. Keep going. Don't give up. Yes, this is ridiculous. Yes, this is outrageous. Yes, Jesus still loves us. No, God has not abandoned us. Yes, God remains faithful. No, I can't make sense of how people can claim they're following Jesus and say, do, *or support* such things. No, it isn't just "mean talk." Yes, we need to love them. Please do not give up. I need you. We need one another to get through this.

Speak up. Take courage. Have faith. Trust that God is doing more than we can see right now. Trust that grace matters and following Jesus means loving one another *and* loving our enemies.

Help me to live this.

1 Grace Frees Us To Try

I'm overwhelmed by everything going on. I need to understand my part in it and let go of all the responsibilities I'm taking that are not within my power. What do you see as your responsibility in this crisis? What parts of that are realistic? What parts depend on God's strength? What parts are just not your job?

Jesus gives us a big job. Massive.

"Love one another."

"Love your neighbor as yourself."

"Love your enemy and pray for those who persecute you."

Jesus gives us such impossible tasks we either give up, become fakes, or find strength deeper than our own.

Grace means we don't have to make ourselves perfect at loving others. We just have to love.

Grace means we don't have to fix everything that is broken, either in ourselves or in this world. If you take your car to the mechanic, you expect that professional to return your car to you repaired, no longer exhibiting the problem, *fixed*.

Grace means God has not made us mechanics. We face problems bigger than we can repair.

I have a friend from college who used to turn her stereo up to drown out the bad engine noises from her malfunctioning car. It became a metaphor among us for choosing not to acknowledge problems, our own or the world's. We don't get to follow Jesus and do that.

But grace means we face the problems and do what we can, accepting our personal limitations, limited resources, and imperfections. We need faith that God will work through us *and* do what we cannot. For us, "faithful" means we do what we can with the strength and love God gives us and then accept the grace that God still loves us when we fall short—or even fail—at this massive job.

Grace *also* frees us to try our hardest, with all our strength and all our heart, because we leave the results to God. When our family lived in Nicaragua, we wanted desperately to break the cycle of poverty in our barrio. We failed to do that. We loved our neighbors, imperfectly. We helped a friend leave an abusive relationship. We loaned a friend money to start a motorcycle repair business. His business is still going and he supports his family better than he could before.

We did not alleviate poverty in *Anexio Buenos Aires*. It wasn't our job to fix it but it was our job to try. God gives us grace for our many failures there. When I say "Grace means we don't have to fix it," that is the opposite of "We don't have to try." If we claim grace as our excuse not to help, not to lift our hand—"I know I'm supposed to care about children who were seeking asylum being hurt, but God has grace for me"—we have twisted and abused God's grace. Grace frees us from worrying that the problem is impossible or that we're almost certain to fail. Grace frees us from paralysis to act. God doesn't ask us to succeed. God doesn't ask us to fix it.

Jesus commands us to be faithful and love.

What feels overwhelming to you right now? How can you approach it with love, seeking only to be faithful, knowing you can't fix it?

Jesus, I'm overwhelmed by our global climate crisis and how our country keeps going in the wrong direction. I'm overwhelmed by this administration's corruption and cruelty. I'm overwhelmed that we have locked asylum-seeking children in cages at our border. Please help me to accept that I can't fix these and give me strength and courage to do what I can to change them, today.

2 I Don't Want to Hate

Hatred is a dangerous, potentially toxic emotion. It also makes me feel powerful, which I prefer to feeling weak and vulnerable. Have you found yourself hating anyone? We're all angry at what's happening. We should be. How does hatred feel different than anger for you?

"I have decided to stick to love… Hate is too great a burden to bear," Martin Luther King, Jr. declared.

I love this quote. I want to make this decision.

But.

But every single day I am tempted.

Throughout my life I've had people who get to me, people whom I have a terribly hard time loving. In fact, sometimes I've looked back and wondered if, at each stage of my life, a new person stepped up to take that role. I'm being facetious, of course, but not entirely. It troubles me how much I've struggled to love certain people.

Now, though, I'm tempted to hate an entire group of people. I'm tempted to hate our leader. Every day. I don't want to hate them. I want to obey Jesus. I want to believe and embrace King's quote and make some once-for-all decision, which is how he seems to phrase it. "I have decided." There. Choice made. Done deal.

I don't want to hate people because I know hate eats us alive. I know Jesus calls us to love, even our enemies, and warns us that calling our brother or sister "fool" (raca) is equivalent to murder. (Matthew 5:21-25)\

I don't want to hate because I know God can work through loving my enemies. I know God can work in my heart when I choose to love and, somehow, reach that enemy with my feeble love.

But.

But they mock and call names. He mocks a reporter with a disability. Every single time I see his expression and the way he bends his arm at that awkward angle to impersonate a man who has a palsied arm—a Pulitzer Prize winning journalist, no less—I feel such anger I want to hate him. I do. And I've seen that exact image several hundred times since he did it in 2016. A high school friend—a real friend—immediately jumped in to defend this, claiming he was misinterpreted, he was just saying the reporter had a cringy, whiny voice. He was just mocking him and mimicking his voice. I feel angry every time I describe that.

I know King is right. I know Jesus tells us the truth about love. I feel hate trying to dig in and take root. I see so many others reviling and disdaining and I agree with the substance of their criticism, and it is *so* tempting to join in. The spiteful laughter feels good, in a bad way. I see and hear all the hatred and vitriol flowing from his supporters and I want to hate them right back. I'm tempted. It makes me ugly, it twists me into whom I do not want to be as a Jesus follower, as a human being, as a beloved child created in God's beautiful image.

Every day I battle this. Some days I embody God's love and empathy and this urge slips to the back where I can almost ignore it. Other days, in the face of a new outrage, it leaps out, front and center, and I'm expending enormous energy to resist.

Resist.

I have decided to stick with love. Every single day, sometimes every hour, I decide. Jesus said "Love one another as I have loved you." In this resistance, I have to resist returning hate for hate or trying to defeat this evil with hate.

Jesus, free me from this hatred. Set my heart free to love. Give me more of your love and help me to want it, even when loving feels weak. Help me to love my enemies. Help me to love others as you love me. Show me how to speak against this evil in love, without falling back into hatred. Make me more like you. Help me stick to love.

3 Love Your Enemies and Pray for Those Who Persecute You

I've spent a disproportionate amount of time trying to understand how we got here. Even now, I still can't quite believe it. I've gone around and around again, trying to listen, trying to make sense of how anyone, especially Christians, can continue to support things I find both appalling and antithetical to Jesus as I understand him. It makes me feel like I'm taking crazy pills.

At some point, many opposing this administration started shouting, "Why bother even trying to make sense of it? They aren't 'trying to understand' us! Screw this 'find common ground' talk! They're evil and we just need to defeat them!" Sometimes it's been expressed in even stronger language. Sometimes I've thought these things.

Following Jesus confronts so much in us that feels "normal" and "natural." I believe we are made in God's image and that image, though at times warped and skewed, remains inseparably part of us. We can't shake off how God made us to reflect love any more than we can make ourselves unlovable to God. We can reject and deny them, but they don't go away. Part of me wants to hate my enemy and avenge myself on those who persecute me. That feels "natural." Jesus leads me in the opposite direction.

If we defeat our enemies by hating them and retaliating with worse than they gave us, we have stopped walking with Jesus. Jesus still loves us but we're not going in his direction. If we decide, "They don't deserve our understanding!" we may be correct from a political or cultural perspective. But we don't seek to understand others because "they deserved it." We give grace because we *receive* grace, present tense. We give grace because following Jesus means spreading grace in the world. In the words of Francis of Assisi's prayer, "O Divine Master, grant that I may not so much seek to be understood as to understand." Francis makes no mention of what others deserve.

Trying to understand others who mistreat me feels wrong when I'm angry. The words taste bad, like bile coming out of my mouth. I prefer to repay them in kind. But Jesus confronts that in me.

"Do not repay evil for evil." (I Peter 3:9) "Bless those who curse you." (Luke 6:28) *Even when they deserve evil,* Jesus did not bother to add, because if they've already cursed you and given you evil, *of course* they deserve it! Certainly they do in our score-keeping minds. Grace means we have received love we did not deserve; following Jesus means we offer love others do not deserve.

Honestly, I've never before felt like I have so many enemies as I do right now.

We Jesus followers sometimes play down having enemies, because "enemies" sounds so bad and un-Christlike. We have people who bug us, people with whom we disagree, "extra grace required" people. If we're honest—okay, if *I'm* honest—often I don't love them, I just avoid them. That's why we need to call them something other than "enemies." I'm not disobeying Jesus because that's just someone who "gets on my nerves." Sigh.

Right now, I experience the population who unreservedly support this administration as our enemy. Brutal honesty, these are not people merely "getting on my nerves." They are supporting and working for things I call evil. They contribute to powerless people getting persecuted. But calling them "enemy" does not represent a defeat for me. Having enemies does not mean I've stopped following Jesus. Jesus told me I'd have enemies. He's more honest about it than I am. He said "Love them."

If I deny that these people are my enemy, I let the anger and even hatred take up residence in me. When I acknowledge that I have enemies—and yes, some of them are dear friends and family members—then I know how to respond. I may not like it, but Jesus makes it clear.

Just to make certain *I'm* being clear: we do better to acknowledge having enemies and try to love them than deny having enemies and continue hating them.

Identifying people as "enemies" does not erect walls or draw battle lines between us and them. Sadly, those are already in place. Following Jesus means we will do what we can to love and pray for them, believing Jesus loves them more than we do. In fact, we believe Jesus loves them like Jesus loves us.

When I know I have enemies, I seek to tear down walls and cross battle lines, at least the ones in my heart against them. Okay, I don't magically or automatically do that, but I hang out with Jesus and Jesus keeps lovingly bringing it up and suggesting steps I can take.

I hate to admit this to you, or even to myself, but I believe the most dangerous part of this crisis for my soul is that I will dehumanize a huge portion of the population. I'm tempted to this, little by little, and every bit of it feels justified. "You believe this is a hoax?" "You think it's *all* a conspiracy?" "Fake news?' But he said those things *himself*!" Rage at each new destructive legislation and executive order, each new, unqualified "acting" director, the growing list of identified and proven lies, each nasty, name-calling tweet, the images of his supporters gleefully chanting slogans. Then I start savoring the anger: the mockery by talk show hosts, the memes and unflattering photos on social media, the endless stream of political commentary. After stewing in all this, I get into an argument with someone who wholeheartedly believes everything they've done is for "our" national good, that person speaks dismissively of my intelligence and—*boom!* "You and *everyone like you*."

Or simply, "You people!"

I can't go there. I suspect that could cost my soul. Jesus pulls me back from that precipice, not by telling me, "There, there, don't get so upset," or "It's not so bad," but with a much stronger tug. "Pray for them. Love them. See them as human. See their need for grace. See *your* need to show them grace."

None of what Jesus says here feels "natural," but that's because my anger warps my judgment. God's image in me is not warped. God's image in me is to love others, not because they deserve love but because God *is* love. Jesus pulls us back from that cliff because our hatred can make us ugly. Jesus will love the unlovely—us—until his love brings out our beauty. I don't see that beauty in this administration's die-hard supporters. But God sees that beauty

11

in me. Therefore, I know it dwells in them, too.

Jesus, make me a man who loves as you love. Show me who my enemies are —help me to admit that they are—so I can love them and pray for them. Save my soul from this justified-feeling frenzy. Help me not to lump together and stereotype. Help me not to dehumanize people you love. Send people my way so I can love them as individuals rather than making a nameless population the enemy.

4 We've All Lost Friends

What relationships have been strained during this crisis? What relationships have been broken? Do you have hope for reconciliation?

It's not a Civil War (and, God-hear-our-prayer, won't be) and I don't want to overdramatize our divide, but we've all lost friends. Sometimes people lose friends over politics and differing views, but we've *all* lost friends through this time. Some of us have severed relationship with family members or been cut off. Paul writes to Timothy, "If it is possible, as far as it depends on you, live at peace with everyone." (Romans 12:8) I wrestle with this all the time. "As far as it depends on me" if I keep my mouth shut and never speak up about the evils I see happening every day? "As far as it depends on me" if I nod and just say, "Hm," every time someone starts expressing hateful, racist views about people living in poverty who have thrown themselves at our mercy?

I don't know where the line is. In fact, I try *not* to live my life following Jesus dictated by "lines." "Do not taste, do not touch!" has no power to restrain sin in my life and does not lead me to godliness (Colossians 2:21-23). Therefore I'm not looking for lines to stay behind to keep me "safe from sin." Sin is the urge inside me to do things that will hurt me but that I'm willing to do because I like the payoff. There's no line I can draw to keep away from myself. As U2 sang, "Where can you go to leave yourself behind?" When I try to establish rules to make myself good, I stop listening to God and move from love to legalism. Instead, I need to follow Jesus into life and have his spirit set me free from wanting to destroy myself.

I think Paul wrote "if it is possible" and "as far as it depends on you," to Timothy, both conditional clauses, because Paul knew not everything could be within Timothy's power to control. Perhaps Paul also considered that Timothy would have to speak up for truth and refuse to to lie or pretend. Jesus followers in the Roman Empire must have faced that choice often.

I cannot be silent in the face of the injustices raging around us. Let me clarify that statement: as a Jesus follower, I *must not* be silent now. That would be sin.

I never want to rule out completely any possibility of reconciliation. Having said that, someone I love dearly was married to a narcissist and I have no scenario in my mind that would make me cheer for her to reconcile with him, much less marry him again. I don't know exactly why you've lost relationships through this divide, but the patterns are predictable. For me, I had to choose between 1)speaking up for those I care about who are being abused and 2)staying silent so certain friends would not reject me. Eventually, I had to accept that I could not reason my way through these conflicts. My efforts were answered with disrespect, criticism and, increasingly, questioning of my character.

I needed to pull back from one particular friend in order to love them still. I do hope we can reconcile, eventually, but I had to stop getting new wounds while trying to heal the older ones. I don't imagine our rift is all the other person's fault, but I reached the point at which I needed more time and distance to heal and even *begin* to forgive—and our disagreements over current events have only intensified.

If you feel alienated from people you have loved, you are not alone. If you hear, "Adults don't lose friendships over politics," well first, *Ha!* Have you read history? Any of it? Second, "If it is possible, as far as it depends on you" is a good guideline. As far as you are able without compromising your faith, without finding yourself siding with the oppressors through your silence, without taking abuse that God does not desire for you to keep enduring. Yes, we are called to suffer in some circumstances; no, we don't indiscriminately allow people to abuse us and spiritualize that as "suffering for Jesus." It isn't. Allowing other people to sin against us without boundaries or restrictions hurts them and us. As I said, I can't offer you lines and rules. I grieve with you over the friendships and even family relationships we've lost in this mess. I can only encourage you—and me, once again—to pray for healing and restoration, but not settle for false peace nor be shamed for rejecting that false peace. Peace can't come at the price of our integrity. If we stay silent when we know by the spirit within us

14

that we must speak out, that is false peace.

We pray for real peace: the *shalom* of reconciliation, the *shalom* of justice and truth.

God, I'm sad for our lost and broken relationships. It shouldn't have to be like this and I grieve that it is for so many of us. I'm grateful for the friends in my life. Help me to bring your shalom *into this world, to be at peace with others when it is possible and to trust you when it is not. Give me hope that we can reconcile someday. Keep me from deceiving myself when I have sinned and want to excuse that as necessary. Please don't let me settle for false peace or be unfaithful by remaining silent when I must speak.*

5 Name-Calling

Have you been verbally attacked over a political position? Has someone questioned your integrity, your faith, your character because you've spoken up? What names have friends or strangers called you?

I could write forty or fifty reflections on "I know they're doing this, but we shouldn't do this back." I hate that our culture is so divided that we have "we" and "they" in such stark terms. But I've been called some pretty nasty names in the past four years. When I had an article on children seeking asylum go viral, I got genuine hate mail for the first time in my life (if you don't count junior high).

It's so tempting to use denigrating and derogatory language. I don't go around calling people malicious names in "real life." Any name-calling I'd be likely to do would be in jest with friends. If I like you and feel comfortable joking with you, I'm much more likely to give you a teasing nickname. My close friends from high school and I still call one another "goon." If I dislike you, I'm more careful how I address you. I resist the temptation to hurt you under the guise of "I was kidding." These days, I feel like I'm reviewing childhood principles of decent behavior and civility.

"We're calling them names among ourselves, not to their faces. Where's the harm?"

In me. That's where I see the harm. I want to be clear, I've done this, far more than I like to admit. Again, it offers a certain satisfaction to vent one's frustration. I, for one, have a lot of frustration built up.

But name-calling does more than vent frustration. Why does Jesus equate one who calls brother or sister "fool" with one who commits murder? (Matthew 5:22) Most of us would never dream of committing murder. I suspect we're willing to understand that teaching as hyperbole and maybe not dismiss it, exactly, but set it aside as "Oh, I should keep that in mind." One could argue that Jesus meant not to call someone "fool" to their face, meaning "do not tear the person down." According to this logic, that makes behind-their-back name calling okay, or at least not as bad. Here's the whole passage:

"You have heard that it was said to those of ancient times, 'You shall not murder'; and 'whoever murders shall be liable to judgment.' But I say to you that if you are angry with a brother or sister, you will be liable to judgment; and if you insult a brother or sister, you will be liable to the council; and if you say, 'You fool,' you will be liable to the hell of fire. So when you are offering your gift at the altar, if you remember that your brother or sister has something against you, leave your gift there before the altar and go; first be reconciled to your brother or sister, and then come and offer your gift. Come to terms quickly with your accuser while you are on the way to court with him, or your accuser may hand you over to the judge, and the judge to the guard, and you will be thrown into prison. Truly I tell you, you will never get out until you have paid the last penny. (Matthew 5:21-26)

Of course, we have a month—or a lifetime—of reflections here. But we know Jesus means it. Anger damages *us*. Insulting and name-calling take us where we do not want to go. Without wading into the issue of hell, we have to read this as a serious warning. Jesus wants to protect us from self-destruction; this is one route we take to destroying ourselves.

Name-calling dehumanizes the other. We always dehumanize our enemies. To treat someone as the enemy, we must first take away their right for us to empathize.

Here Jesus' command becomes radical for everyone who would follow him. We automatically, almost instinctively dehumanize our enemies because we may have to kill them. We may have to kill their children. We may have to commit atrocities against them that we would never want done to us. (I know, we're categorically denying we could ever do such a thing. True. We have our police and army do it for us. The result comes out the same.) But Jesus confronts this, both by commanding us to do to others as we would have them do to us *and* by commanding us to love our enemies. My urge to crush my foe becomes a choice: I can follow my urge or I can follow Jesus. I cannot do both.

Of course I can think of lots of rationalizations and excuses why what *I'm* doing doesn't fit with this prohibition. I don't really have enemies. I don't really hate anyone. This is tough love. I'm good at ducking Jesus' commands. Too good.

But if I'm honest with myself, and with you, I know that when I call my enemy nasty names, I'm not seeking to love. I'm not doing to them as I would have them do to me.

I know they're calling us names, but we shouldn't call names back. *I* shouldn't call names back. I know my heart and I know Jesus. I know he's right. I want to follow him, not my hateful urges, because those urges would destroy me, as sure as the hell of fire would destroy me. If there is hope for my redemption, and for redemptive love to transform my enemy, I must let God's love disarm my destructive urges.

I have to end with this: I'm not discussing what anyone "deserves." I deserve much worse than I will get, because God has grace for me. I'm not talking about turning a blind eye or closing our mouths to evil. We'll address those.

Jesus, I repent of my name-calling. I want to believe what you say. Help me to love my enemies. Give me strength to resist the temptation to revile those I oppose. I don't know how to break down these walls, but I know I need to stop this. Guard my tongue and change my heart. Amen.

6 Exhaustion

I'm tired.

Most often during these years of this crisis, I feel angry or tired. Usually I cycle between the two. I hear of some new outrage daily and get angry, which motivates me to speak up, pray, and look for constructive responses (as well as curse, rage, and complain). But this wears me out. My adrenal gland is getting overworked. I'm exhausted, emotionally and spiritually. I'm writing this book because I know many of us feel exactly this way.

In cliché Christianity, we solve this by "letting go and letting God." In my experience, cliché Christianity fails not because it's untrue but because it doesn't work that way, certainly not that simply. In other words, we've taken a truth and oversimplified our application. Only rarely are they flat-out lies. Jesus *is* the answer. I *do* need to let go and let God.

I'm facing exhaustion. I live a comfortable life, much easier than when I lived in Nicaragua. I got tired there, too, but this feels different. To be clear, I also felt helplessly angry at injustice in Nicaragua. I couldn't fix it there, either.

But I need to make changes and I need to decide how engaged I can stay. I can't make all this go away. I can't pretend it isn't happening—to be clear again, I *can* pretend it isn't happening, which epitomizes my privilege, but as a Jesus follower I *mustn't* bury my head in the sand and decide "not that much skin off my nose."

So how do I read through the list of environmental protections that this administration has stripped away and "let go?" How can I hear from another friend who suffered sexual assault, remember that we have a President who has twenty-five *different* women accusing him of sexual assault, that we confirmed a Supreme Court Justice directly in the face of a woman stating that he held his hand over her mouth while he attempted to rape her...and "let God."

I have no idea.

But here we are.

The rate at which these outrages come pouring out, along with the sheer volume of what's been done by our country and in our name, make my knees buckle. And that's not yet addressing the behavior and words of those who support what's happening.

I. Am. Tired.

This is how much of a mess I am right now: a few days ago I was driving and a red pick-up in the next lane over started to switch lanes and then wildly swerved back again to avoid slamming into the Honda that was already there. Blind spot, I'm guessing. We've all been there. I was the car behind these two. The car that almost got sideswiped sped up and got out of there. The driver who was trying to change lanes, now running out of space before we turned to cross the bridge, signaled. So I slowed way down to let him in—I was already going slower from that cold sweat down my spine when I thought the cars right in front of me were going to crash. But I definitely went out of my way to let him in and he knew it. After he changed lanes, he stuck his full-sleeve tattooed arm out the window to acknowledge the kindness.

And I got teary.

His simple acknowledgement of my act, a tiny little drip of decency in a raging hurricane sea of hostility, and I choked up.

Kim, preparing for her school year of distance learning, has worked 14-hour days the last couple, and when she describes what she's going to have to pull off to teach this year, it sounds like two full-time jobs. The freaking NBA protested the police shooting of Jacob Blake. No playoff Wednesday or Thursday. I was trying to express how overwhelmed I felt with this latest shooting—and the shooting after that, a 17-year-old killing two, injuring a third—when the WNBA, NBA, as well as some MLB and MLS teams, brought their games to a screeching halt to defend and advocate for black lives.

I'm profoundly encouraged to see this because these are people with a major platform and powerful voices. If you hope for non-violent protests, these are the epitome of speaking up non-violently.

Of course, there's much more than this going on. In case it slipped by you, we're in an election year. As of today, 184,000 have died from COVID-19, a horrific number which is still likely underreported. Somehow arguments against wearing masks to prevent its spread continue.

"Look around, look around at how lucky we are
To be alive right now." You know, from *Hamilton*.

In 2020, it's tempting to sing that sarcastically. But then with so many dying of this virus, that feels like sacrilege, doesn't it? The pandemic began raging in the U.S. in March. It's only August. A friend survived it but his wife describes

> It's been a month since he came back home after his ordeal of 103 days in the hospital-rehab isolation venture due to COVID-19. His days are mostly spent in bed due to the ulcer wound that continues to heal. He still has no sensation in his feet, and unable to walk yet.

He's younger than I am. We keep praying for him and his family.
I have a friend who is an ICU nurse. She just gave me the update on her hospital.

> We are able to care for 16-18 patients, but it is a strain on our staffing to do so long term. We are attempting to hire experienced ICU nurses, and we have 8 nurses in the residency program training to become an ICU nurse but that takes 3 months. Our nurses are working overtime, and we have currently acquired the most traveling nurses that we have ever had. Travelers are an expensive way to go because they cost the hospital much more than hired staff. (The hospital pays the nurse and the travel company). We currently have 14 or 15 travelers! Normally, we hope to have none, but occasionally have hired 2-4. This current trend is unprecedented. It is a good thing I live in an attractive place to work and play, so we can attract travelers to our area. I am sure some areas in the country struggle with attaining travelers.

This is a response I got to a recent blog post. Please pay attention.

I have noticed that I am thinking about death much more lately. Some of that probably has to do with me and many friends being in our 70s, 80s. Feeling less and less time, Your words help me a lot. And this upcoming election scares me to death. I have actually found myself thinking of how to leave life if 45 wins. But then your words help me feel love for my family, friends, and associates. And I smile. I pare down the size of my world. Then I can handle that.

We're in crisis and I'm not the only one feeling it. So when a stranger acknowledged me, just that simple arm-wave, the universal signal for "Thanks," I got emotional.

In contrast to the driving incident, that same outing I stopped by the local mall on my way home because I desperately needed the restroom. Twenty feet from it, an employee told me, quite harshly, "The mall is closed. You need to go the main exit and leave. *Now.*" I wasn't the only non-employee still there, by far. It wasn't two hours after closing. And I go to that mall so rarely that I don't actually know their closing time.

"You're ugly and your mother dresses you funny!" I did *not* say that to him, but the urge came welling up, hard. Now come on, Mike. He's an employee mopping the floor after the mall is officially closed. Yes, he could have spoken nicer to me, but he has *every* right to want to go home from work when it's time. And it's not his fault how his mother dresses him. I spent my drive home (this was my second failed attempt to stop for a bathroom) uncomfortable *and* working through the steps of putting myself in his shoes. Because to do to others as we would have them do to us, we have to identify and empathize. Getting angry is easier than identifying and empathizing. SO much easier.

Here we are. Small acts, not even necessarily of kindness but simple civility, make me cry. Small acts of incivility hit harder than they should—than they normally would, if I can even remember back to what "normal" felt like. I read about people getting angry at being asked to wear a mask and physically attacking the requester, whether a teenage employee or a stranger. I want to judge the heck out of them—and I do think that's a horrible thing to do–but I'm also aware that I, personally, am running on approximately zero margin. I'm not excusing horrible acts or awful decisions; I'm acknowledging that we all have more going on right now.

I have. I recognize both of these tiny incidents as symptoms to which I must pay attention.

So here are my takeaways:

1)It's right to react strongly to injustice and horrors going on around us. I'm not feeling bad that I'm feeling bad about all this. When I stop caring, I'll worry. I'm questioning anyone who doesn't carry these things heavily. Knowing how to retain peace and centeredness in turmoil is not the same as indifference.

2)That means we have to increase our self-care, too. As my friend described, we may have to pare down our world. If we can't handle all that's going on, we *must* make healthy choices to step back and breathe, increase our capacity for what we must handle, limit or mitigate the damage we're taking if at all possible (not always the case), and, in my humble opinion, keep speaking up and standing up.

3)How do we keep loving in the midst of *this?* It seems as if people are getting worse. Behaving worse, attacking more viciously, reasoning even poorer or less (which frankly I didn't think possible), and somehow nevertheless *more* convinced of their rightness and righteousness in all of these. And I mean it looks like this to folks on both sides of the political spectrum, looking across the divide. I know with absolute certainty I'm not the only one feeling "those people" are harder to love right now. Therefore, we need a soundly biblical understanding of "love" to keep loving *right now.* Love does not mean pretending that evil is not evil. Even forgiveness demands calling sin and darkness what they are and calling them into the light. Love never means calling evil good. Love does not mean turning away from sin and choosing harmony over truth. Martin Luther King, Jr. wrote, "*True peace* is not merely the absence of tension: it is the presence of justice." If we can follow this truth in love, seeking God's *Shalom* through loving our neighbor while confronting injustice…

Oof. It's exhausting. I'm emotionally stretched to my limit. I know that. I want to acknowledge that. I want to respect my own limits and yours. I believe everything I just wrote, I will try to live this, *and* I'm exhausted.

This is all I'm telling you today. Many of us feel exhausted. If you roll your eyes and call me a "snowflake," that's fine (especially if I don't hear you). But if you can relate, I'm offering you this: **love is still the right path**. I know it's ridiculous to get teary when a stranger just arm-out-the-window thanks you for letting him merge. But trying to listen to God's Spirit, I took that to mean small acts of love mean *even more* right now.

Yesterday, I was driving a little fast and then saw a boy, maybe nine, standing with his bike at a crosswalk. I stopped abruptly, which inspired the truck coming from the other direction to stop even more abruptly. The kid looked nervous and hustled across before either of us ran him over. So I rolled down my window and called out to him, "Good job!" smiled, and gave him a thumbs up. Safely on the opposite sidewalk, he smiled back and returned my thumbs up. Small acts mean *more* now, I'm convinced. Loving others while we're near our breaking point (or feel that we are) is still where we encounter God. Loving our enemies when they have doubled down and committed themselves to enemy-like behavior will always be the path of life. If by some miracle you are reading this and disagree with all my positions and think of me as your enemy (and maybe God's), well, then this applies between you and me.

Some things we have to say not because we'll change others by saying them but because not saying them will change us. I'm not going to lose my soul in all this. I'm not going to become or give in to the hate I'm beholding right now. I know people deny that it is hate, and maybe it's fear masquerading as hate. That's not for me to judge. I just know I'm not going there. Grace still applies and I'm still loved by Jesus in spite of all the bad stuff I think and say and do. I'm not righteous, I'm saved by grace, and I refuse to let myself believe that I am good and others are evil. I refuse to turn a blind eye.

"I have foresworn myself. I have broken every law I have sworn to uphold, I have become what I beheld and I am content that I have done right!"
shouts Elliot Ness in *The Untouchables*. Great line, strong movie, but no. Absolutely not. I also refuse to fight against hate with hate and let myself

become the hate I stand against.

As Bono sang,
    They say that what you mock
    Will surely overtake you
    And you become a monster
    So the monster will not break you[1]

I'm encouraged that I get teary at minuscule responses. I'm glad God's spirit still moves in me to offer children affirmation. Many of my thoughts and inclinations right now are not encouraging. I mean, genuinely concerning. You may see some of those in yourself, too.

But God is with us and, by God's grace, we will not become what we behold. We will keep trying to speak—and live—truth in love.

"Be imitators of God, as beloved children, and walk in love, as Christ loved us." (Ephesians 5:1-2a) These words have never sounded more concrete and tangible to me, because the choice never before looked this clear.

I had written this and then, that night, found out Chadwick Boseman died, and I couldn't even. It felt like a gut kick, or lower. That news both underscored the premise of this reflection—there's so much and it's so bad—and doubled me over. We need leaders and role models, people of character and courage. We can ill afford to lose those we have. Go with God, Chadwick, and thank you, Black Panther.

Jesus, many of us have hit our wall and have little or nothing left. We're exhausted. Give us strength. Help us to persevere. Please protect us from getting calloused or numb, guard our hearts from hating others, and lead us to rest well and take better care of ourselves as we endure this. Help us to keep loving.

U2, "Peace on Earth"

7 I Need You To Admit You're Wrong

We're in a political crisis. I'm trying to convince you of the danger. You do not see it.

I need you to admit you're wrong.

This is probably the most unhealthy response I have to our current situation. Of course, "You" in this sentence is the person, whether friend, family, or non-acquaintance, who cannot and will not see what I see. When I state it like that, with no context, it sounds horrible. I sound horrible. I sound egocentric and arrogant, as if I think everyone has to understand everything exactly as I do or they are wrong and blind.

But I'm not a narcissist. No one has accused me of being one in my fifty-one years of life (to my face, anyway). I'm wrong often and I try to admit it freely. In fact, friends accuse me of "reckless transparency." I choose to be open about how screwed up I am and value vulnerability over self-protection. We show people God's grace when we let them see our weaknesses and how God works through us nevertheless.

Therefore, I have to step back and recognize that what we're all facing is a qualitatively—perhaps categorically—different problem right now. I'm thinking "desperate times require desperate measures." I could make a list, this second, with no need for no notes or reminders, of one thousand things that appall me about what is happening in our country right now.

Everything has changed—but that's one of the things we see that others don't. So all our healthy boundaries and principles of good relationships still apply. That even in itself feels crazy. How can "normal" still apply? Very early in this administration, people who opposed it started making comparisons to Nazi Germany. Objectively, I get why those who support this administration got upset and reacted strongly to that. But I also think some of those comparisons apt; some who have made them lived through and *were eyewitnesses to* Nazi Germany.

26

Right now, I'm in the midst of a months-long political dialogue with two friends from high school. We have stayed not merely civil but friendly, mostly, even through moments when we've felt extremely frustrated with one another. I wish, I *wish* all political discussions could go like this. Yet even in this dialogue, I've felt like I may be going mad because I present evidence and exhaustive, reliable, sound sources but one can't see what I see. Can't or won't. Conclusions that appear inescapable to me, he still escapes!

If we were in my house, you and I, and I heard a noise that suggested someone might be breaking in, I would tell you. If I heard more noises that reinforced my suspicion, I would hope you would hear them, too, but failing that I would describe them to you, urgently, and assume you might share my concern. How long would this process have to go on before I got frustrated that none of my evidence of a break-in persuaded you? In this situation, I'm not sure I could say, "Well, to have good boundaries, we need to understand that others may not agree with us and accept that with grace." I see other considerations, like our lives being in imminent danger. Or how my wife might feel, coming home to a house robbed of our belongings or me injured? Would I just shrug it off and agree to disagree?

Probably not. I think I would proceed to respond to the emergency regardless of your belief or disbelief. I'd have to. I wouldn't have a good category for why I had failed to convince you—you're intelligent, you understand cause and effect, you're not in league with the thieves—but I'd have to let all of that go. Yes, it would be easier to deal with this crisis if you *were* helping, certainly if you were acknowledging the reality of what was happening to us, but failing that, I would have no choice but to address it myself and sort out our failure to communicate later.

I understand that the people who disagree with me think this analogy doesn't fit—but that's precisely the point! We believe we are in a terrible crisis and people who don't see that *don't see it*. I can't make them see it. I've tried many approaches and am still trying.

But for my spiritual health and my sanity, I have to let go of my need for them to see what I see. I have to let go of my need for them to admit they are wrong, that yes, there is a burglar in the house.

I think I struggle most with our disagreement over morality. From my perspective, we're not merely debating politics, *certainly* not "politics as usual." People whom I respect, whom I believe have a genuine relationship with Jesus (as much as I can discern), support or turn a blind eye to atrocities that I *know* Jesus abhors, as much as I know anything about God. I offend them horribly even by stating that.

But precisely because of the depth of the conflict, I *have* to make this between me and God, not me and those people with whom I'm arguing. Jesus loves them. Jesus loves me. I must let go of this need to make them admit something they will never admit. I can't make that a condition of our friendship, and especially not a condition of my grace for them. We may not be able to continue in the relationship, but that will depend on factors beyond disagreement, even over something so crucial as this.

I'm not good at "just leave it to God." I'm much more like the dog who can't stop chewing on the bone, even when there's barely any bone left to chew. Even when the bone happens to be my ulna...or my spleen (I know, not a bone; it's the image I always get for how compulsively I obsess on things). But our current situation makes leaving other people to God's grace imperative, both for the sake of the friendship and for my mental and spiritual health. I don't have the emotional reserves right now to keep having fruitless arguments over whether we just heard breaking glass, much less keep offering patience and grace in these arguments, much *less* offering patience and grace when I'm getting insulted or abused in return. I still need to attend to the burglars.

When I feel betrayed over disagreements concerning this President and his administration—when, not if— and when I've expressed my view as clearly and firmly-but-graciously as I can, I must be willing to leave them and their response to God. It's now between me and God how I will love them, how I will accept our disagreement, and especially how I will trust God for the future. I'm not solving this crisis by making them believe what they don't; I *must* trust God, whether we solve this crisis or not.

To spell out this contrast: When I keep it between me and the other person, I still want to change their response. I can't let it go. I won't stop trying to "make them see," to reason with, convince, and persuade them. Maybe berate them. Perhaps harangue them. If necessary, even... You get the idea. But that is *not* loving them. That is sinning against them and imagining I have power to "fix them" that I don't and never will—nor should—have. I think I'm describing Boundaries 101, but in the light of our current crisis, where so much is at stake, it's tempting to suspend certain boundaries, as if we're calling a State of Emergency for how we handle our relationships.

But we can't. In fact, suggesting that is just another way of saying "the end justifies the means." Jesus followers don't get to claim the end justifies the means, *especially* when people would become the means.

To be one hundred percent crystal clear, I am not saying we stop speaking up for what is right and against what is wrong. We cannot. Other people's disapproval must not shut us up and we should *expect* to pay a price for refusing to be silenced. The burglar is in the house.

I am saying I have to trust God more than my own (imagined) power. I am saying to be a man of peace, I must offer peace, and grace, and kindness, even with those with whom I disagree over such life-and-death matters. "Blessed are the peacemakers." I don't want to say that as mere pithy punctuation. I want to work for the *shalom* of God's Kingdom. I have to let go of my need to make others agree.

Jesus, I'm trying to respond faithfully in this crisis, but fruitless arguing isn't the way. I'm terrible at letting go and trusting you. I prefer my illusion that I can make people get it. I need you to help me to become a peacemaker. Help me first to know your peace, then to stand for peace while offering your grace to people I want to persuade. Jesus, help them to see what I can't make them see. Show me where I'm wrong. God, have mercy on our country. In Jesus' Name.

8 Matthew 25 and Loving Jesus

[I wrote this while in Nicaragua. Instead of rewriting it in present tense and current circumstance, I'm sharing it as a perspective I had in the midst of an environment very different than what most of us experience in the U.S., even in the poorest neighborhoods. This shapes and informs my perspective.]

It's always difficult to talk about poverty and injustice.

First, no one likes to hear from someone who sounds self-righteous. I certainly don't. When someone boasts about being the best, or gives any impression of bragging about superiority, I immediately question everything that person says. To me, credibility plummets. So now we live in an impoverished community, which is very different from where most of our (other) friends live. I'm trying to find the balance of speaking what I know without coming off as saying, "NO ONE understands poverty like *I* do!"

Second, I constantly feel like I'm failing here. That's the truth and I'm not seeking pity or even reassurance for this. I'm doing my best to live faithfully where God led us, but neither my insomnia nor my feelings of failure have budged in the time I've lived here. Thus, far from feeling like an expert, I second-guess myself about everything I say concerning the conditions and the people we live next to here.

Third—and this is not a good reason—people don't seem to like to hear it. I totally relate that we don't enjoy reading things that make us uncomfortable, especially when there is some suggestion we should *do* something about it. I've learned that the vulnerable, bleed-a-little-in-front-of-people sharing resonates, that someone may benefit when I talk about my own issues with depression or doubting God. But offering insights from my strengths is a lot less popular, especially when those include challenges. So I shrug and keep praying.

That brings us to Matthew 25. Christians, the evangelical ones certainly, proclaim that we have a *personal* relationship with Jesus, that we want to know Jesus more, to be closer and more intimate with him. If you scan the lyrics of "contemporary" evangelical worship songs, they talk about this stuff (and seeking for God to be with us in our trials) more than anything else.

> Then the king will say to those at his right hand, "Come, you that are blessed by my Father, inherit the kingdom prepared for you from the foundation of the world; for I was hungry and you gave me food, I was thirsty and you gave me something to drink, I was a stranger and you welcomed me, I was naked and you gave me clothing, I was sick and you took care of me, I was in prison and you visited me." Then the righteous will answer him, "Lord, when was it that we saw you hungry and gave you food, or thirsty and gave you something to drink? And when was it that we saw you a stranger and welcomed you, or naked and gave you clothing? And when was it that we saw you sick or in prison and visited you?" And the king will answer them, '"Truly I tell you, just as you did it to one of the least of these who are members of my family, you did it to me." Matthew 25:34-41

If we say we want to love Jesus and Jesus says, "Here I am," it makes sense that we would try to be there, too. Assuming we mean what we say.

We can encounter Jesus in many ways. Of course we seek those, as well.

But nowhere else in the Gospels, which give us the direct words of Jesus, does Jesus describe his immediate presence like this. I experience God more in nature than in anything else; stick me on a mountaintop and I will certainly "see" God, every time. That's just how I'm wired. God gave us five years of living in the mountains where I could walk out my door, turn right, and immediately be hiking up into the hills. It was beautiful and I loved it and felt that God was giving me an extended (albeit challenging) retreat. Then God led us to move to Nicaragua and into an impoverished community.

Why would God take me out of the place where I most easily and readily experience his presence?

Well, two obvious reasons quickly come to mind: it's where Jesus said he is present—among those hungry and thirsty—and Jesus' Kingdom work is about bringing justice and transformation—*we* needed to be closer to Jesus and have him transform us so that we could be more part of his work. Though I struggle with feelings of failure here every day, inarguably God *has* transformed us through our years in Nicaragua.

Mother Teresa described this as

> Seeking the face of God in everything, everyone, all the time, and his hand in every happening; This is what it means to be contemplative in the heart of the world. Seeing and adoring the presence of Jesus, especially in the lowly appearance of bread, and in the distressing disguise of the poor.[2]

Jesus is present in the distressing disguise of the poor. He says so. One of the worst dangers of Christianity, and one we all fall prey to and from which we must repent, is picking and choosing which of God's truths we like and follow and which we'd prefer to ignore or explain away. There are some passages we'd prefer to use our lowlighters on, just dim them right down so we don't have to deal with the discomfort and distress they cause us.

> Why do you call me "Lord, Lord," and do not do what I tell you? I will show you what someone is like who comes to me, hears my words, and acts on them. That one is like a man building a house, who dug deeply and laid the foundation on rock; when a flood arose, the river burst against that house but could not shake it, because it had been well built. But the one who hears and does not act is like a man who built a house on the ground without a foundation. When the river burst against it, immediately it fell, and great was the ruin of that house. Luke 6:46-49

But following Jesus means following what he says, especially what he says to do. Grace is meaningless if we just do whatever we feel like and expect God to bless it. That isn't the grace Jesus offers. Grace is that, by God's love and kindness, Jesus forgives us and makes it possible for us to live our lives to the fullest. God's grace means that, instead of leaving us to destroy

---

2   Mother Theresa, *In the Heart of the World: Thoughts, Stories and Prayers*

ourselves, Jesus makes us partners in this work of restoration and redemption that we call God's Kingdom. We get to be part of lives becoming whole and so full of God's love that they become contagious—beginning with our own.

I am friends with people here who I would never have known if we had stayed on our mountain in Washington. God has changed us through these relationships, through our encounters with him here, exactly where he said we would find him. As I write this, there is a little girl with a cough and a runny nose who is resting on our couch on our back patio. She loves me, in the way that sometimes almost-two-year-olds just decide they love you, whether you deserve it or not. She starts calling my name, loudly, almost every time she sees me and sometimes when she doesn't see me. Today she is feeling awful and has been screaming a lot because she's miserable…and almost two.

This isn't some moment of lighting-flash revelation, some epiphany. If she feels much sicker, we might give her mother and her a ride to the clinic. Because we have some partnership-friendship-neighbor-family relationship with them, we look out for each other. I don't mean merely that we provide for them or pay for things; it doesn't work like that. They watch out for us as much as we watch out for them. I can't fully explain how it works, but it *does* work. I can't explain how Jesus is present in refugees and prisoners and this little girl, but he says he is. I call him, "Lord, Lord."

By his grace, I'm doing what he tells me.

Guilt bears rotten fruit. Conviction, in which God helps us to see what needs to change and gives us the power to make those changes, that brings life and joy and freedom. I have no idea how you are responding to Jesus in this area of loving those in "distressing disguise" and I'm certainly not judging or serving as travel agent to send you on guilt trips.

But I believe Jesus is who he says and does what he says and *means* what he says. So I will ask you:

Where do you find Jesus in his distressing disguise? Where is he asking you to join him? Where does *he* want to be with *you*?
Jesus, help us to recognize you in everyone, even in your disguise. Help us to love you as you come to us.

9 A Horrible Day in the Neighborhood

When I was a tween and beyond, we made fun of Mister Rogers. His name was not linked in our minds to kindness and compassion, but to simplistic, naive, pretend-everything-is-happy goody-goodism. Raise your hand, right now, if you remember *Mister Robinson's Neighborhood*. (I know, you might be on your Kindle or your phone at the office or coffee shop or, God forbid, driving your car. What the heck. Raise it anyway. And *put down your phone while you drive!*)

Eddie Murphy spoofed Mister Rogers on SNL and gave us a glimpse into a very different neighborhood than the one we'd grown up on. Do you know how popular *Mister Robinson's Neighborhood* was? Nike paid NBA star David Robinson *beaucoup* bucks to do a series of commercials also entitled "Mr. Robinson's Neighborhood" (get it?) in which other basketball stars like Charles Barkley, Gary Payton, and Rudolph Firkosny (haha) showed up at the door and they would make a quick joke and show you the Swoosh Stripe. You know you're popular when they make a parody of your parody.

You also know you're popular when they make a parody of the parody about you.

As a teenager I thought I knew nearly everything[3] and that my jaded, cynical, reality-is-ugly-but-at-least-I-*get*-it perspective made me superior to those who lived in a fantasyland of goodness. Even though I wanted to make the world a better place (while getting famous and rich), I was clear that people are generally awful. I mean *Brave New World, Lord of the Flies, 1984, Animal Farm* awful.

---

3 By twenty-five I did, in fact, know everything. That started to get shaky with Rowan's birth and went severely downhill from there, leading me, at my current age, to hang out with Uncertainty as my near-constant companion. Uncertainty is a strangely comforting bud to hang out with, once you stop fighting her. But hey, aren't we *all* nicer to hang out with when the other person stops attacking us constantly?

The brilliance of Mister Rogers–which I completely missed when I knew everything but get so clearly now that I know so much less–is this: Mister Rogers was *not* pretending that every day was perfect and thus beautiful; he knew that some days are horrible and could be beautiful, anyway. No, better than that: he knew we could *make* them beautiful, anyway.

The humor of *Mister Robinson's Neighborhood* is that an innocent-sounding narrator describes and encounters nasty features of inner city life ("The word for today is 'Racist'"). But the brilliance of *Mister Rogers' Neighborhood* is that he acknowledged the painful, sometimes horrible aspects of life–for children!–and continuously spoke a message of hope, that we can be okay in this real world. We can make this painful real world better for one another.

Rather than putting on a fake smile or burying our head in the sand, Fred Rogers "preached" that we can smile, for real, and still look our problems in the eye. The very act of offering our smile to people in pain *while standing with them in their suffering* is an act of courage and compassion.

Think I'm making something deep that wasn't? I'm not.

> When I say it's you I like, I'm talking about that part of you that
> knows that life is far more than anything you can ever see or
> hear or touch. That deep part of you that allows you to stand for
> those things without which humankind cannot survive. Love
> that conquers hate, peace that rises triumphant over war, and
> justice that proves more powerful than greed.
> - Fred Rogers

Dostoyevsky wrote *The Idiot*, arguably his most personal and intimate novel, about a loving, compassionate, authentically *good* character at the center of a culture that valued none of those things. Many of the other characters take Prince Myshkin to be simple-minded and foolish, an idiot. The think does and says such things because he doesn't know better. Ready for this?

I thought Fred Rogers was an idiot.

But I was.

The beauty of this, to me, is that people, generations, *loved* Mister Rogers. Loved him and recognized him as a hero in our midst. In *A Beautiful Day in* *the Neighborho*od, the main character, based on the journalist Tom Junod, suspects that Fred Rogers must be fake, must have an angle, must be playing people with that "goodness and kindness" act. I just thought he was a fool. We were both wrong.

As Dostoyevsky depicted with Prince Myshkin, many people felt drawn to Fred Rogers, but unlike Dostoyevsky's embodiment of good in a corrupt culture, Fred Rogers remained grounded all his adult life, did *not* go mad, and offered his message of hope in kindness through the end of his life.

In 1969, Fred Rogers had a scene in his show in which he and François Clemmons shared a wading pool, both taking off their shoes and sticking their feet in together. That image on a children's television show, a white man and a Black man sharing the same pool, was a radical act of racial reconciliation in 1969. Fred Rogers, whom I mistook for a fool, was a social justice warrior.[4] He confronted systemic, generational sin in our culture and fought for human rights: racial equality, education, disability rights, mental health, peace. These are the things that make for *shalom*. You'd better believe he's one of my heroes and a role model for us to emulate.

"Be careful then how you live, not as unwise people but as wise, making the most of the time, because the days are evil." (Ephesians 5:15-16) What if the days are evil *and* we seek to make them beautiful? I've wrestled aloud in my writing, over and over, with how we confront these evils running rampant right now *as* Jesus followers, in his spirit of compassion and *shalom*. "Do not repay anyone evil for evil..." "Do not be overcome by evil, but overcome evil with good." (Romans 12:17, 21)

I have a better idea how to do that now.

So please excuse me, I need to go binge some Mister Rogers' episodes. *Jesus, thank you for Fred Rogers. Thank you for the people who have modeled grace and love in our broken, hurtful world. Let us not be overcome by evil but overcome evil with good. In your name. Amen.*

---

4 I know that term is used as an insult (I recognize the belittling, mocking tone from when I used it on others as a teenager). I'm reclaiming it. I'd love to be worthy of the title. I think following Jesus requires this, in whatever small ways we can. If we're not fighting *for* social justice, what is the alternative?

10 When a Life Matters

I'm going to try to approach this from a different perspective. If you're willing, come along and we'll think through this together.

Do lives objectively matter, in the cosmos? *Why* do lives matter?

When we say that "A Life Matters," it begs the question "To whom?"

In the big, physical-existence only picture, the answer is "no." Not really. Go back and check the size of the universe. Then check how many people will die today. Happens everyday. More people die, more people are born, the stars shine and go supernova and black holes swallow up light and does any of it really "matter?" No. It just is. I'm describing an answer to the question if we don't immediately ask "To whom?" Based on the best scientific evidence, we're a blip, a blink, just passing through with no impact and no real relevance. Then we're gone, decomposing in our physical form, switching to other forms of matter–so do we matter? Yeah, the pun is almost too strong to resist. But I will.

If I tell you that you matter, I mean you matter *to someone*.

The great and shocking truth of Christianity–and this is a belief, not a scientific fact I can prove for you–is that *bigger than the universe*, greater and older and infinitely more than the universe, exists a God who answers that question, who in fact initiated that question so you would know the answer.

Genesis 1, describing the chaos that was pre-creation, addresses the ancient belief that existence is without order, ultimately threatening and either utterly indifferent or even malicious toward human existence. The writer of Genesis conveys, "No, God who created everything brought order and, from the beginning, bestowed both value and purpose on humanity." We are all made in God's image to share God's value and God's purpose–and God, we learn, *is* love. We matter to God. God loves us. God loves us *and* shows grace to all of us, meaning God doesn't stop loving us or love us less when we hurt others or ourselves.

Now if you don't believe in God's existence or you reject that a creator God loves us, you have to answer "To whom?" differently than I have. Humanity has attempted to answer that question apart from God. I won't recount all those various attempts; I'm taking the long way around, but not *that* long. I'm just pausing here to say you still have to answer the question.

Okay, from the abstract to the very personal and immediate: you live as if some people matter more than others. You might say "All people matter equally," or 'All people matter equally to God." Perhaps this means all people have a *right* to matter equally or "All people have equal value" (which is really a different issue). But none of us live as if all people matter equally *to us* because that is impossible. We talk to some people and not to others. We spend money on some people and not on others. If one person is rushed to the emergency room, we drop everything and go; others are rushed to the emergency room and we say a prayer...or simply don't notice at all. Remember, we're talking about lives "mattering" to us, not whether lives have value to God. Who matters to you? I think it's probably self-deception to say "Everyone matters equally to me but I just pay attention to certain people and not to others." If you got the news today of someone's death, you would not respond equally to that news regardless of who died. Neither would I.

When I lived in Nicaragua I realized that Nicaraguan lives did not matter very much to most people living in the United States. It was a bizarre experience, yet probably one shared by nearly everyone who lives abroad and comes to love the country and people of their adopted home. These lives, Bismarck and Juan Ramon and Mileydi and Exequiel, were abstractions to my friends from my native land. I had the strange honor of trying to make them real to other people I love.

But I'm not claiming I'm special, I'm just describing my experience. If a person in Burkina Faso dies tonight, that person will be an abstraction to me. I don't know that person. If I somehow found out and it was a little girl, I would feel grief in that general, abstract way we do over the world's pain, injustice, how children should not die before their parents. But in the past week, I learned that Manuel, who lived in our barrio—no, we lived in his—

and who watched out for us as *his* gringo family, died. Manuel was an alcoholic. He treated his body horribly and we knew his life expectancy couldn't be terribly long. But he was younger than I am and now he is gone and I grieve. He matters to me. Of course he didn't matter to you as much as he matters to me if you never met him. When I told you he was an alcoholic, he may have mattered to you a little less; you might now think, just a little, in the privacy of your heart, "he deserves what he got."

But people can *not* matter to us when we know them, too. Jesus tells a parable about a man living in poverty named Lazarus and a rich man named…"rich man." Unsettlingly, Jesus doesn't give the rich guy a name. But the rich man steps over Lazarus at his gate, ignores Lazarus's suffering and needs, and continues on with his comfortable, pleasurable life.

We're not like the rich man, of course. At least, I'm willing to bet we have all told ourselves that we're not and gathered our reasons to back this up.

"But Mike, you're being unfair! A life can matter to me even if I don't interact directly with that person! I can value a person's life from a distance. I can say that person matters without having to feed him or dress her wounds or clothe their children."

Hold that thought.

My life matters. To whom? It matters to me. I value my own life. I feed myself and exercise and try to take reasonable care of my health. I also try to enjoy myself, to do things that give my life meaning by my own measure, and to be a person I can bear. I try to love others even when they don't love me, to show kindness to those who refuse to show kindness to me.

My life matters to me *because* my life matters to God. I can't say the following with certainty—I don't have a control group to test my hypothesis— but I believe I would not be alive if I didn't matter to God. We usually phrase this as "Because God loves me." In the mysterious, inexplicable ways of God, not only does God love me but Jesus has taught me that the very the purpose of my life is to do what I can to help others know that God loves them, also. You. Nicaraguan friends. Ultimate players. My kids. Strangers on the street.

Can lives matter without purpose? They can, but I think it's harder for us to accept. We still matter to God if we feel we have no purpose at all, but part of Jesus's conveying to us that we matter is inviting us to join in God's purposes. Those are big. Reconcile the world to God in love (as opposed to at gunpoint). Redeem and restore all that we've damaged with our hate and violence and our disfiguring of creation. Build *shalom* community. In fact, I would say our purpose and our love, both given by God, cannot be taken away. Even if we lose our ability to do *everything*, God still works through us to love and heal. That's grace.

We convey that others matter by affirming their beloved-ness. We recognize and call out their reflection of God's image, by which I mean that they are both loved and capable of loving. The more abstract this is, the less it touches people. The more specifically and truthfully we can tell and *show* people they are loved, that they have purpose and value and significance *to us*, the better chance we have of helping them to know that they matter.

Yet numbers work against us. Can you love a thousand people? A million? Can you love twenty people? Twelve? Only two?

Of course, the answer is that we can love different numbers of people in different ways. For how many people would you rush to the hospital? That is one very specific expression of love. That you would not rush to the hospital for everyone does not mean you don't love everyone, but again, you don't love everyone equally. We have limits. We could smile at everyone we meet, but we can't listen well to every person we meet (believe me, I've tried). We can share our food with some but not with everyone. We choose.

As Jesus followers, we trust that God, who is infinite, can and does love everyone while we seek to love those within our reach. Even for those within arm's reach, we have to choose how we can love them. We who are finite do our small part and believe God uses our small part for the whole, what we call "God's Kingdom," God's overall work in the world.

Complicating these matters, I'm both sinful and broken. I love imperfectly, even when I'm crazy about the person. Some people I flat don't like, or don't enjoy, or don't respect, or don't accept. Jesus literally commands us to love *everyone*—including enemies—and not just abstractly—not the empty gesture of "thoughts and prayers" without real prayer or active love—but specifically to love them as we would want to be loved.

Of course, my failures and shortcomings in loving others don't mean they are less lovable. Nor that they matter less to God. But it means little for me to say people matter and yet demonstrate by my action or inaction that they do not.

Our church has a sign above the door that says, "You matter to God, so you matter to us." That's our calling that we recognize from Jesus. Jesus says they matter, so they matter, and consequently we seek to help them to know that they matter, to show by what we say and do and *don't say* and *don't do* that we affirm their value. To God. To us.

Therefore, if we have a movement within our country insisting that certain people matter, of course we have the calling to affirm this truth. Jesus makes that clear. I have never, in my thirty-plus years of following Jesus, felt the need to convey to anyone that they matter less. Have I needed to confront some people's pride and ego? Of course. But not their value. Not that they matter to God or to me.

Going back to abstracts and specifics, of course every person in the whole world matters. But how many people feel specifically loved or valued by my declaration that "everyone matters?" Notably, our sign doesn't say "Everyone matters to God so everyone matters to us." Of course we believe that and try to live it. But my calling, now and in each moment, is to help *you* know that *you* matter. You won't feel that more if we tell you, "Yeah, everyone." It *is* everyone. But you have to hear that it's *you*. YOU matter to God. So YOU matter to us.

In Mark 5, Jesus went rushing off with Jairus, a very esteemed and powerful man in his culture, because Jairus begged Jesus, "Come, heal my daughter!" But on the way, Jesus got stalked by a woman. She came up close to him—violating her culture's laws, by the way—and touched his clothing. Stalker. This touch healed her. You may not believe that, but I do. But the story isn't that Jesus magic-healed her without trying; Jesus stopped and asked, "Who touched me?" Remember he was rushing to heal a dying girl with the girl's father, a man who mattered very much within the hierarchy of that culture. Jairus's daughter mattered very much to Jairus, Jairus beseeched Jesus for help, Jairus mattered to Jesus, and Jesus charged—until this. This lowly, sickly, impoverished woman (all strikes against her) did not believe she mattered to Jesus *at all*. Not even enough for him to lay eyes on her. *I can just touch him*, she thought, *get healed, and he won't ever have to see me or know I exist.*

Jesus stopped. Jesus demanded, "Who touched me?" Peter said, "It's a crowd. Everyone is touching you." Yep. Everyone. Everyone matters. Jesus didn't ask that. "Who touched me, for I felt power for healing flow out of me." What? But the woman knew she was busted. She fell to her knees in front of him—have you ever actually dropped to your knees before another person? I don't think we can even quite get how demeaning, how lowering this act might be. Jesus spoke with her. He raised her up. He listened. He affirmed her. He told her, "Your faith has healed you. Go in peace."

Then, and only then, did he resume hurrying to the emergency of Jairus' little ten-year-old girl.

I've heard people say, "Jesus didn't heal everyone who was sick in his time. He didn't help everyone who was poor." It's like they understand that Jesus imposed human limitations on himself yet also don't understand. Or conveniently forget. Jesus loved and modeled loving. He didn't come so that he could directly heal and love everyone—*even though he certainly loved everyone*— but so that we could learn how to love as he loves us and spread this love, person by person, throughout the world. He showed love all the way to and through his death, and to his followers' shock, even after his death through his resurrection. He atoned for our sins in that death and imparted his life to us in that resurrection.

Yes, now we're there. Gears shifting.

If someone tells you their life does not matter, as a Jesus follower you have one clear answer. If someone tells you, "I'm worthless, I want to die," you may not be able to change their mind but you know with certainty that they have worth, love, meaning, value. They matter.

If someone tells you, "I feel as if I don't matter," you have an answer. We know our calling. We know why they matter. We can address what in their life makes them feel they don't matter.

If Lazarus says to you, "The rich man steps over me. I don't matter," you must tell him, "The rich man is wrong! You *do* matter, God loves you, and that indifference and neglect by that nameless wealthy person cannot negate your value. You matter!"

If people feel like it's debatable whether or not they matter, our part, always, *always*, is to affirm how much they matter to a loving, grace-extravagant God, and to us, imperfect and finite but loved by God and learning to love like God. If we love others as we want to be loved (i.e. the way Jesus commanded), we know we want to be reminded of and upheld in our value. We may do that poorly for others, but we know the truth; we know our calling. If Black people tell us they experience that their lives do not matter within our culture or legal system, why on earth would we do anything other than affirm with them that their specific lives *do* matter?

As Jesus followers, we affirm to people that *their* lives matter. Any response that waters this down, or questions or attacks why they bring up the question—imagine answering someone who is suicidal, "Why are you even talking about that?"—works against what Jesus did with the woman he stopped for, what Jesus does when he stops for us. As Jesus followers, we can only be on one side of a discussion someone else raises about whether or not their life matters:

Yes, you are right. Yes it does. *Your* life matters.

Jesus, give us strength to stand with those whom our culture, nation, or world say do not matter. Help us to work against and change systemic injustice and racism. Help us not only to say but to live that Black lives matter. Let us respond to those who feel they have no value or are not valued by loving them and affirming their value. Amen.

11 Being Right Versus Being Loving

[The next three reflections all address disagreement. They consider different approaches to handling these conflicts in which we find ourselves. I hope they complement one another and help us think holistically about our confrontations and how we love others *and ourselves* in these interactions.]

Here's the thing: you can be right all the time and still be a horrible human being.

When Jesus followers use the word "believe," we mean an action, not a set of abstract truths to which we consent. Therefore, "Believe and you will be saved" does not *mean* "Agree to this information and your soul will know life."

People ask me, all the time, "Why are Christians so awful?" Christians and people who are not Christians alike ask. That's not a fun question to hear. It's even less fun because a lot of people who label themselves as "Christians" do atrocious things and claim Jesus as their inspiration, justification, or moral covering. Of course this isn't true of all Christians, and of course some who call themselves "Christians" aren't, and believe it or not even I'm not foolish enough to make blanket statements about who I think is or isn't.

Jesus said, "Love one another as I have loved you." (John 13:34) He said, "By this everyone will know that you are my disciples, if you have love for one another." (John 12:35) He also said, "Love your neighbor as yourself," (Mark 12:31) and, just to make sure he'd covered the range, "Love your enemy." (Luke 5:44)

Then there were all the times he said, "Make sure you're right."

No one will know we are Jesus followers who God's love by our winning arguments. *Absolutely* no one will know we follow Jesus when we behave like buttheads in our arguments.

Being right, biblically, is not as important as being loving.

I'm going to say that again: Being right is not as important as being loving.

Some will immediately jump on their high horses (meaning they must be good high jumpers) and shout "*Truth! Truth!* You can't compromise truth!"

I'm not talking here about truth. I'm talking about our seemingly unquenchable need to prove ourselves right.

Three things remain, Paul writes in I Corinthians 13. Remain after what? See how it begs that question? Three things endure, last, still matter after everything else has passed. What are those three things? Faith, hope, and love.

Of these, faith might be the one related to knowing and expressing the truth, but most of us realize that living by faith or practicing faith requires action and obedience, not mere assent to information nor the ability to debate that *I* have the right information. Both "belief" and "faith," in biblical language, require action. But by no stretch of the imagination (at least not mine) can I render "'faith remains' means dying on this hill of my own rightness."

The greatest of these is love.

Of course, none of *us* do what I'm describing. You aren't feeling convicted because while we all know "they" do this, *we* certainly don't.

So let me tell you what *I* do: I think less of people when they argue too much and I judge people who won't stop arguing. Sometimes, in my mind, I call them names. Sometimes, those names move from my mind to my vocal cords.

You know why I do this?

Because I'm right.

So let me dig in further: when I say this, I don't mean "If you disagree with people, love requires deciding that they are right and you are wrong." That isn't love. Neither does love require staying silent in every discussion.

However, neither does speaking the truth substitute for love. I know (too) many people who believe that if they just speak the truth, God will open people's minds, convict their hearts, and therefore the only thing that matters is "speaking the truth in love" meaning "I just have to make you hear what I have to say." If *every* time I speak the truth it's guaranteed to help people, then "speaking the truth in love" simply means speaking the truth, which is, *de facto*, loving.

What's the strongest way I can say "That is wrong?"

I suspect this view explains how we get people equating "I prove I'm right" with "I'm being faithful to Jesus." I see people label this "Standing for the Truth" or "Refusing to Compromise."

I'm not even wading into whether we turn out to be wrong when we think we're right. That, as they say, is another kettle of fish. I'm saying that we may be better off staying silent than speaking the truth without being loving. When people seek to start arguments with me on social media, most often I simply don't respond because I see no fruit coming from the argument. If I can't figure out a way to respond in love, I try to shut up. I will tell you, doing this hurts my ego, wondering if they think they're right and have silenced me with their brilliance (when I happen to think they're dead wrong). But I'm not seeking to preserve my ego; that would require different priorities than Jesus calls me to.

To drive this home: You can "win" an argument and push people further away from Jesus. You can be right and demonstrate the opposite of God's love for them. You can do that in Jesus' name.

Getting back to me for a moment: I have strayed too far from staying centered on love. When I witness someone arguing, and I disagree with their view, do I think "how can I love that person?"

If that seems extreme, I have this sermon I'd recommend on loving your enemy.

The answer may simply be "Shhhh."

The answer may be praying for someone whose views oppose mine so strongly that I would label him or her "an enemy."

Or it may be disagreeing respectfully.

Can you really be right all the time and still be a horrible human being? If we define "being right" as "having an accurate understanding of a specific truth," then yes, absolutely. Knowing the truth and living the truth turn out to be widely, sometimes wildly different things. "Living the truth" means being changed by the truth we live. If you can't see yourself changing—or have someone you trust see that change for you, if you're a harsh self-critic

—growing in grace, humility, love, generosity, kindness...then it's possible your "truth" may be merely the hammer you wield.

I know that sounds harsh. I just see too many people swinging hammers and feeling self-righteous about the assault.

God, let us be known by love and not assault.

I want people to ask me, "Why are Christians so loving?"

God, help us to be loving. Keep us from using our words as weapons or our arguments for violence. Help us want to love even more than we want to be right. Help us all to be more loving, especially when we disagree. In Jesus' Name. Amen.

12 The Argument for Arguing

[This can be taken as the counter-balance to "Being Right Versus Being Loving." We have to speak up.]

I try to look at issues from a little different perspective. When people dig in on whether "Black Lives Matter" or "All Lives Matter" I want to say, "Wait! You keep using this word. What do you mean by 'A life *matters*?'" (Reflection 10). We take for granted that we're using common terms and definitions. Usually, we aren't.

I'm reconsidering the value of arguing. I've had some really good discussions about it and friends have challenged me to think of it from a different perspective. My views are changing. Here's what I've got right now.

First, I always want to begin with grace. We can disagree with people and still show kindness and grace. I can disagree with you and not make you my enemy. We can disagree and still be friends. This doesn't always happen, as "We've All Lost Friends" acknowledged, but it *can*. We hold out hope.

The argument against arguing is "No one ever changes their minds, it only leads to hostility, and therefore you're wasting your time." Somewhere implied within that is "...and those people are ~~bad word~~ jerks and you can't reason with them."

I have felt this, strongly. I won't tell you that everyone has good intentions but is simply misunderstood nor that if we all had patience and used our inside voices we'd have a group hug and share s'mores and put all our differences behind us. That's bull. Some people aim to hurt you. Some even feel entitled to do so because [insert rationalization here] or they honestly don't care how you feel because what they're saying/doing is more important than your feelings. Or the relationship. Or you. You can refuse to be someone's enemy but you can't force them not to treat you as one.

Jesus followers seek to value every person, however obnoxious or antagonistic or evil. Why? We believe God loves literally everyone and every single person, no matter how obnoxious, antagonistic, or evil, carries the image of God and the spark of God's light. On my best days, I believe that.

That does *not* mean we endure any and all abuse from others. Sometimes Jesus calls us to suffer for others and sometimes Jesus calls us to *suffer others* because they need love even though they are damaged and will hurt us. The view that we only surround ourselves with those who like, affirm, and agree with us *and* the view that we have to endure and absorb every abuse to "suffer for Christ" are both counter to Jesus' call for us. I would call them both partial truths that become very unhealthy if we make them absolute truths. Loving our enemies doesn't automatically require taking whatever hurt people throw at us. When they are sinning by hurting us, simply permitting that helps neither them nor us. "Boundaries" is not a word found in the Bible, *per se*, but healthy boundaries are inherent in biblical love for ourselves and others.

We *do* need to surround ourselves with people who will love, affirm, and challenge us. Friends who speak truth to us. Show us grace. Tell us how beautiful we are because they can see God in us when we can't. If we don't have enough support, if we don't participate in some form of community, we cut ourselves off from a central stream of God's love.[5] If you don't have strong support, I'd say address that before you figure out arguing, priority-wise.

When I'm talking about "arguing," I mean disagreeing strongly with someone who does not and likely *will not* agree with us. I don't mean "discuss" or "dialogue" or "converse." I mean argue.

My first impulse has been to say "don't." If you know you're never going to agree, and we also suspect no one changes their mind, what is to be gained?

But we live in this strange age. We live in a world that is connected (and disconnected) on social media platforms and in which many of our fellow citizens—and many of our friends—receive their news and form their opinions

---

[5] Community is also a place we can get horribly wounded and abused. I wish that weren't so, but the gathered sinners do sin and it does us no good to deny it or pretend otherwise.

through what they see on social media. The recent scourge of conspiracy theories related to COVID-19, which quickly picked up massive momentum in spite of the obvious facts to debunk them (if a video trending on Twitter is found to have 80% of it's viral circulation coming from troll farms and Russian bot accounts, that's a giveaway), serve as a perfect example. People whom I know, love, and respect wrote to ask me, "How do you know this isn't true?" Honestly, that's a good, open-minded question and also indicates how crucial is our responsibility to fact-check and investigate.

Why? Why do people want to believe these voices over those with vastly more experience, expertise, and legitimate credentials? Well, that's certainly a book of its own. We're fearful in the time of our pandemic. We want to believe that it isn't as bad as we're hearing, that the cure is coming soon or already here (though maybe being hidden or suppressed). We've been duped enough by government allowing big business and false science to inform us.[6] Once burned, twice shy.

Our reality is more complex than we'd like it to be. We want simple answers and we want them *now*. We're freaked out that science is a trial and error process even when lives are on the line, even when our children's lives are on the line. We want to skip the trial *and* the error part of the process, which makes us susceptible to those who disregard scientific method and happily supply "the answers."

We've also devolved into a society that has chosen sides for everything, including who will inform our reality. "Fake News." How loaded is that term now? It's become shorthand for "I *must* distrust everything this source reports." What's worse, both major parties have also promoted identity politics, i.e. one's political views are not a collection of positions taken from across the spectrum to align with one's beliefs and values, but "I *am* my party because that other party wants to destroy the USA!" Identity politics is perhaps the single-worst hindrance to reasoning and drawing conclusions based on facts for those who have the capacity to do so. (I acknowledge this as a danger for myself, as well, and one that I must guard against.) Going

---

6 Did you know smoking cigarettes was not harmful to your health up until 1999 or 2006? I'm being facetious, of course. Big Tobacco lied to and deceived the U.S. and worldwide public for how many years, with hired scientists to back their falsehoods?

back to our example of COVID-19 conspiracies, if the "other side" is trying to debunk a conspiracy theory, that makes some of us that much more inclined to believe it–not based on facts or scientific research or any kind of proof, but because everyone knows "they" are bad and liars, regardless of what debunking evidence they produce.

I have to conclude we simply do not have the luxury of ignoring "ridiculous ideas." If by "arguing" we meant solely "two people facing off, each trying to prove a point while refusing to hear or consider the other's perspective," I'd rush to tell you "Yeah, don't. Please avoid that argument, save your time and energy, and don't further damage the relationship if there's anything to be spared."

In my discussions with trusted friends regarding arguing, we noted several competing values to consider. Engaging in argument with someone who will never listen, much less change their mind, is frustrating and exhausting. If you're (lucky) like me and take every criticism, insult, and slight to heart, you can end up fixating on it for days. On the other hand, people are paying attention. A surprisingly large number of people have told me, "Thank you for what you say. Thank you for speaking up." Some of them do not feel the liberty to speak up themselves and some say they get so much backlash for what they say that it isn't worth it.

These represent the silent readers, who know better than to respond directly and get caught in the crossfire, but who are still trying to make sense of everything that is going on or make sense of a particular issue. They don't wave their hands or give away their stealth positions very often, but they're there. If everyone rolls their eyes at the preposterous conspiracy theories but no one bothers to rebut them "aloud," then these claims go uncountered.

Say this happens with the tobacco industry. Obviously we can tell that cigarettes are causing cancer but *they're* still denying it, still spending billions to convince people it's a lie or make the scientific findings seem hazy--often people don't need to be convinced, they just need an excuse not to be believe what would be inconvenient. But if the only voices people hear are the denials of truth–and believe me, Big Tobacco paid a lot to make that denial loud–then it's much easier for people to get (and stay) fooled. Then, by staying silent, perhaps we're complicit in their getting fooled.

51

As with so many things, I can't give you a simple "yes" or "no" answer whether we should engage. Reality check: I can chase my tail all day on this stuff. I confess to having done so before. Turns out I gain little whether or not I catch my tail and I can't get that day back.

I have a very close friend, Geordie, who has changed his position entirely in the past five years (not my doing). He reminded me just a couple days ago that dialogue and well-reasoned confrontation in love can and do have an impact, as he himself is living proof.

I also had a weeks-long, exhaustive (and exhausting) discussion with this guy about the President and got nowhere. When he disagreed he would obfuscate or demand my proof and then, when I provided it, ignore it and go on to the next objection. He claimed not to like this President, at least "not the way he talks," but ultimately preferred to vote for him again unless the Democrats ran a candidate with all Republican positions. I learned a lot from that discussion, one of the biggest takeaways being it simply wasn't worth my time. I don't regret entering into the discussion, and, knowing me and my optimism, I would probably do it again. But I shouldn't. Or, when the signs become obvious and inescapable, I should accept them sooner and move on.

I want to add that I still believe in give and take. I know I'm not right about everything. I won't change my mind about this President—he's done too much damage to our country and hurt too many people for anything he does now to turn that around, and I simply don't think it's a good idea to have a full-blown narcissist leading the country—though I do pray for his redemption most every day. But I still appreciate when people can challenge my thinking respectfully (or at least civilly) and help me to broaden my understanding. I want to learn and grow.

So here are my conclusions. As always, feel free to ask questions, share your thoughts, or simply let me know how wrong I really am.

Grace first. Treat others kindly. Name-calling is still wrong, whether or not others do it. At all times I want to remember that God loves and seeks the persons with whom I disagree.

If by "argue" we mean keep disagreeing in private when clearly neither person has any notion of changing and we're doing more damage than good, don't. That one is simple.

Don't let someone abuse or gaslight you. You get to decide when it's abuse or gaslighting.

Consider whether you have surrounded yourself with people who attack your every word or with people who agree with every single thing you say. Find enough support that you can sustain speaking up. Remember that we all need community and strong, healthy community can bear disagreement.

Choose your battles carefully. Choose your battles carefully. AND *choose your battles carefully.*

Watch for when you go beyond speaking up for the truth and begin chasing your tail. Balance your time and emotional investment between remembering that someone is listening who needs your encouragement and that someone else can't wait to tell you how wrong you are.

Balance your choice to respond between your inner conviction to stand for justice and your need for sanity. Don't get sucked into interminable arguments. Say what you need to say. Say it respectfully. You don't have to get the last word. God is faithful.

You have no idea how much your support, your voice, your courage to contradict falsehoods or racism or hate speech or gaslighting or privilege might mean to someone else. They might tell you. They might not.

But *I'm* telling you. **Your voice matters. Your courage matters. Your decency and kindness matter.**

> Remind them of this, and warn them before God that they are
> to avoid wrangling over words, which does no good but only
> ruins those who are listening. II Timothy 2:14

but also

> Speak out for those who cannot speak,
> for the rights of all the destitute. Speak out, judge righteously,
> defend the rights of the poor and needy. Proverbs 3:8-9

I leave you with this: just as I'd rather be excluded for whom I include than included for whom I exclude, I'd rather be attacked for speaking up against injustice than have peace by leaving those experiencing injustice to feel alone. Every time.

Jesus, I need much more wisdom to know when to speak up and when to stay silent. Help. Give us strength and courage to speak when we should and discernment to stay silent or stop disagreeing when we can do no more good or am falling into fruitless debate. I really need more grace for myself for when I screw up or fail at this. Help us to remember that you are faithful and you send us to try, not to be perfect. Let us err on the side of love, especially showing love to those who most need our support. Amen.

13 Intellectual Dishonesty

I feel exhausted by intellectually dishonest conversations.

I'm trying to remain engaged with people who believe differently than I do right now. Throughout my life, I've successfully carried on extended dialogue with folks who follow different faiths, see the world differently than I do, have different political leanings, and even cheer for different sports teams. It isn't always easy—I've been threatened more than once for being a Yankee fan—but it is rewarding. Walls come down when we're willing to engage and listen honestly, meaning listening to learn and not merely waiting until we get to speak, or, worse, to "correct" and rebut.

But I have experienced trying to converse about our current situation much less positively. I'm straining here both to employ "I" statements and to express this diplomatically. I'm not talking about the ugliness of name-calling and personal attacks. We know when people resort to these behaviors that they are responsible for their actions. I mean dialoguing with those who also believe they are trying to discuss honestly. Having unpleasant discussions with people you like, respect, or have known for a long time hurts a lot more when you feel injured by it and you don't know why.

Manipulation is exhausting. Most of us, when we realize we are being manipulated, feel some combination of weariness, frustration or anger, and —paradoxically—perhaps relief. At least I do. Why relief? For me, it's the moment I stop trying to negotiate as if we're both playing fair. When our kids were young, they knew that the moment we detected they were trying to play mom and dad against each other, the answer became "no." Instantly. (Doesn't mean they didn't still try it. Or that we always caught it.) We were no longer having a fair negotiation. So yes, that's upsetting, but it's a relief when I realize, "*Oh*, I feel miserable about this conversation because you're playing me! Ahh! That explains it." That's what I mean by "relief." I now understand that the guilt I'm feeling is most likely not my conscience nor conviction from God's spirit, but the other person intentional pushing my buttons. Of course, it's never quite this clear cut, but the principle really helps.

We call intentionally committed fallacies in debates and reasoning "intellectual dishonesty." Here's a very helpful list of some forms intellectual dishonesty can take.

1. **Arrogance or "I am the messenger of truth"**
2. **Handwaving or "Your views have no merit".**
3. **Unwavering commitment or "I know I am right – why bother arguing?"**
4. **Avoiding/Ignoring the question or " . . . and let's not forget about . . ."**
5. **Never admitting error or "I am/We are right – regardless of your evidence".**
6. **Employing double standards or "Your evidence is unacceptable (because it's your evidence)".**
7. *Argumentum ad hominem* **or "You're a [insert label/stereotype here] . . . and you have a secret agenda"**
8. **Destroying a straw man or "You might say that, but how do you explain . . . ?".**
9. **Ignoring the principles of critical thinking.**
10. **Ignoring [partial] defeat or See Sign #1**[7]

Intellectual dishonesty is a form of manipulation. On my more grace-filled and charitable days, I'm willing to believe that logical inconsistency isn't always intentional or conscious (you don't have to manipulate consciously to manipulate; trust me on that). But here's the problem: manipulation hurts whether the manipulator intended it or not.

I suspect that often in these discussions, people don't realize the fallacies they're committing. So by this definition, they aren't employing "intellectual dishonesty."

But that doesn't make it any less exhausting. It doesn't feel any less manipulative. This is where mocking and meming (is that a verb yet?)

---

7 The only credit I found for this was "A. Robustus" and a broken link for a blog, so credit to A. Robustus, whomever that may be.

becomes awfully tempting, and I mean "a temptation for me to be awful." I've seen ones that lampoon how "they" reason, and of course they're both wryly amusing and a bit relatable, which is what makes a good meme, if that's not an oxy-moron. The issue is not whether they accurately describe some arguments we've had, but whether that generalization takes our hearts in a good or bad direction.

I'm praying hard on this, because it's an area that I find eating at me. But, quite seriously, I think we have a combination of duplicity, un-self-reflective dishonesty, and a lack of grasping the fundamentals of logical reasoning. So here's a simple statement to cut through all the complexity:

If people can't or won't argue right, that doesn't give you permission not to love them, but it does give you permission not to argue with them.

Of course, you aren't required to argue with anyone. The permission I want to give you here—the permission I want to encourage you to give yourself—is to stop trying to play fairly with people who can't or won't play fairly. I don't mean join them in intellectual dishonesty and manipulation; I mean stop. Really stop. Pick your battles wisely. Don't pick this one.

It's okay. Stopping may be the thing you need most. Experience the relief that comes with "Oh, I'm being manipulated and therefore I don't have to play."

I'm offering a reflection, not attempting to teach a class on logic, so I will leave it to you to recognize when others are wielding intellectual dishonesty. It's so tiring, and convincing them of the injustices we see feels so urgent, I think we get sucked into this cycle of trying, getting frustrated, trying harder and/or more forcefully, and then just getting pissed, grabbing our head in both hands and screaming (literally or figuratively).

We were out protesting, holding up signs, my family and I. Twelve of us in our extended family, on the sidewalk by a main road in our small city. Signs that read "Black Lives Matter," "Do Justice, Love Mercy," and "Racism Hurts." A man slowed down in his car, looked at us, and shook his finger in the universal sign of "No, no, no." Dismissing everything, on each sign, as utterly wrong. Something about that gesture stuck with me. Intellectual dishonesty. He's not listening to nor considering our points. And the driving by, obviously taking no time to engage or in any way consider that *he* might be wrong about, say, disregarding "Do Justice, Love Mercy," for example. That's become my metaphor for this experience. I need to say what I must say, what God convicts me to say. The driver's dismissive index finger didn't cause me to put down my "Do Justice, Love Mercy" sign. But neither did I try to chase him down the street to convince him. I laughed. Truly, I did, because it struck me as so ridiculous that he would out-of-hand wipe away all voices and viewpoints contrary to his own—with his hand.

It's easy for me to identify and disengage from this version of intellectual dishonesty—no, you can't dismiss all arguments with which you disagree by mustering the substantive evidence of "I don't like that." How perfect that on the list this is summarized as "Handwaving!" Now I know exactly how that looks. Yes, this is certainly intellectually dishonest argumentation. I can pray for that man—i.e. love him—without arguing with him. May we see as clearly--and disconnect as cleanly from—all who would be intellectually dishonest in our discussions.

We don't have permission not to love them, but we do have permission not to argue with them and not to be manipulated by them.

Jesus, you know I'm terrible at recognizing when people are manipulating me. I get caught up in these arguments too easily. Help us to see it more clearly and to disconnect while still showing grace, rather than reacting only with emotions. Please show me when I'm the one being intellectually dishonest and give me the humility to admit it and repent.

14 Repentance

If my greatest spiritual danger in our milieu is categorizing the portion of our population who disagree with me as enemies, my second greatest danger, and closely related, is letting myself believe that I have done right and they have done wrong.

How easy is that? Hard as I've resisted it, "We" and "They" seems inescapable in this moment. I do think we're right and they're wrong. Even more stark, in many cases I think they support evil and we oppose evil. How short a hop-skip-jump to conclude that I must be righteous and they must be sinners? Yes, I'll always *say*, "I'm also a sinner saved by grace," because I know how bad it sounds when I forget to add that.

But when I think about who needs to change right now, I think about them, not me. I don't think I can overstate the danger this poses for me as a Jesus follower.

Jesus loves us. You, me, and *every* diehard anti-immigration, USA First, "Name even *one* time this President has lied" voter. Jesus loves us equally and Jesus loves us *the same*. By "equally" I mean God does not have maybe just a little bit more love for me than you or him or them; the degree to which God loves us is equal. Jesus loves us "the same," as well; he goes about loving us through consistent means: Jesus atones for our sins, then affirms our movement toward truth and wholeness and convicts us when we step toward falsehood and self-fracturing. We could say "integration" versus "disintegration."

Of course, how Jesus expresses that love looks different with each of us on any given day. When the rich young ruler approached Jesus, Jesus loved him and told him, "Sell all that you own and distribute the money to the poor, and you will have treasure in heaven; then come, follow me." (Luke 18:22) When a leper approached Jesus, knelt before him, and begged, "Lord, if you choose, you can make me clean," Jesus immediately responded, "I do choose. Be made clean!" (Mark 1:40-41) The father in the story Jesus tells in Luke fifteen behaved differently toward his two sinful sons because their behaviors required different expressions of love. The emaciated, pig feces-stinking, rag-clothed son did not need the father to confront him. His father's love for him came in embrace, in being enrobed, affirmed and celebrated. But the father did not run out into the field and throw his arms around his elder son. He didn't call for a robe or sandals. He loved them equally and he loved them the same—both needed to know they were loved, both needed to see their own sin and brokenness, both needed to see beyond themselves. But their circumstances, choices, and attitudes called for very different actions by their father to express his love for them.

Jesus calls people who justify putting children into cages to repent. *Of course* he does. I can see that so crystal clearly and I cannot, for the life of me, grasp how anyone could *not* see that.

Jesus calls me to repent, too. Not just generically because "I'm a sinner." I don't think "generic repentance" exists. Jesus calls me to repent from my particular sin in our current crisis.

I know what they should do differently. What do *I* need to change? That I can't see my sin and need for repentance as clearly as I can other people's sin and their need for repentance sets off every alarm and red flag and bell and whistle I've got left. It should.

I'm not playing nor engaging in sophistry here. My next line isn't "But of course I know that thinking I'm right means I'm arrogant and so I need to repent, too." Those feel like empty words to me.

I know that I've also contributed to our current disaster, I simply don't know how.

I want to blame "them" for everything. That's why this temptation is linked to making "them" the enemy. God does not see them as the enemy and God does not see me as blameless.

I'm not used to seeing myself as the elder brother in the parable. In fact, I hate the very thought of embodying that role. But am I standing with my hands on my hips, right now, furious at them for what they've done and keep doing? You're *bleep-bleep* right, I am! Stick me in a field and the similarity is complete.

60

You see the conundrum.

I need a change of mindset. I don't mean I stop seeing sin by others as sin. I mean I need to take seriously that I am not their judge nor their accountability partner—believe me, they have not asked—and carrying their sin around as my burden, even if only to accuse them of it, can never benefit me or them. It will not lead me to wholeness. It will not draw them to repentance.

If I pray for them every time I think of their sin, at least that would move me godward. I may begin by praying exclusively for their repentance, but I've learned that when I start praying for others regularly, God starts to change my heart toward them.[8]

I also need to seek God more for *how* I need to repent. *Of what, Lord?* I'm certain that the elder brother did not do a "searching and fearless moral inventory" of himself while standing out there, seething about his wretched brother's celebrated return. In fact, I'm going to guess he rehearsed "But when this son of yours came back, who has devoured your property with prostitutes, you killed the fatted calf for him." (Luke 15:30) I know what obsessive outrage sounds like. Again, I relate to this (ostensibly) fictional character much more than I wish I did. I need God to show me, today, how to walk humbly and repent of my own sin rather than review, yet again, the sins of others.

I don't think this will change my position as a resister. I do think it may change my attitude and my behavior as one. King "decided to stick with love." This is one of the decisions I can make to help me avoid hate and stick with love, too. I don't want to join—or even resemble—the elder brother. I certainly don't want to find myself on the opposite side of the the father's argument for grace.

God loves us all the same way, calling us to repentance. God will express his differently, in the manner each of us needs to hear it. I need to open myself, which will require taking my hands off my hips. Consider how

---

[8] I confess that has yet to work for this President, but I'm trusting God and playing the long game. I suspect that my constant impression of how many people he hurts and how much damage he does, with no indication of remorse or acknowledgement at all, has made my heart slow to shift toward compassion and empathy.

different the posture of the elder brother in the field from the tax collector praying in the temple. (Luke 18:9-14) When I see my own sin, I will have more mercy for others' sin, including (maybe especially) those who currently do not see theirs.

Jesus, I repent of my pride and arrogance. I repent of letting myself believe that, the times when I am right, that also makes me better or more righteous. Please show me when I'm standing with the elder brother and on the opposite side from your grace. Give me humility and honesty to see my sin within this crisis and repent. Let me receive your grace for myself and desire your grace for others. Amen.

15 Grieving Our Broken *Shalom*

God created us to live in life-giving relationship with our Creator and with one another.

We aren't there.

Shalom[9] means being in unity with God, being people of holistic peace—peace with God, peace with one another, peace with creation. Reconciled, in harmony, knowing God's love and dwelling in and spreading that love.

We aren't there.

When I describe it this way it sounds ideal and removed from reality. Of course we don't live in this *shalom*. Daily commutes and grocery lines and kids' bedtime routines and grocery lists don't feel like living into *shalom*. It's just, you know, life.

But we grow into *shalom*. We learn to make these small moments holy. We learn to live mindfully. We grow in awareness of God's love for us and how we can offer—or refuse—that love to those around us, including in all those seemingly-mundane activities. I don't consider this ethereal or pie-in-the-sky. Whether in a *barrio* in Managua, a small city in the west Cascades of Washington, or the heart of Manhattan, knowing God and living as *shalom*-makers has the same components. Prayer. Awareness. Scripture study and meditation. Making our work and our friendships part of our sacred space. Creating community. All the pieces that a Jesus follower lives, whatever their location and context.

But our crisis has damaged our *shalom*.

I'm tempted to say "shattered our shalom" (plus, that phrase has such resonance), but God is still God. We have not lost every hint of *shalom* any more than we have lost every trace of God's presence. That would be absurd to say and give all of us (on both sides) more power than we will ever possess.

---

9 I use "*shalom*" both because it's the biblical term and because "peace," our usual word to translate "*shalom*," has much narrower connotations in its popular usage.

We can't wreck things *that* badly. Thank God. We can't destroy God's presence with us any more than we can destroy God's Spirit dwelling in us.

Neither do I want to pretend that we were nearing perfect unity or peace on earth before this.

But our *shalom* together, our fragile peace and work toward reconciliation, does wax and wane, and right now it's so diminished that I have days I'm searching for it and other days I feel blinded and unable to see it at all.

We rightly need to grieve the current state of our *shalom*, in contrast to the *shalom* God intends for us. When people say, "We're so divided right now," I think they're describing a symptom of our damaged reconciliation and peace.

I've quoted many times the statistics of how divided the church is over this administration—and what percentage of the white evangelical church supports it. I'm sure you've seen those numbers. Moreover, I'm sure you've felt their impact in your own life.

I'm not angry because a political side (which I claim not to have[10]) lost an election or doesn't have the majority. I'm not grieving some party's loss of power. I'm not grieving "politics as usual."

If it were that, we would be overreacting.

I want to know God's *shalom* in my being, in my home, in my community, in my church.

The cycle of conflict and antagonism we're caught in, both our nation and the body of Christ within our nation, has not moved us toward *shalom*.

I grieve this.

I'm in grief and have been for three-plus years. I'd like to tell you I've always handled that grief in a healthy way, but of course I haven't. I've failed to recognize it for what it is. I've numbed it. I've tried to escape it. I've scapegoated others for *my* loss of *shalom*.

This leads me to consider both the individual and corporate aspects of *shalom*.

Shalom is a corporate reality that we seek *and* a state between God and I that I can seek and enter and exude.

---

10 As a Jesus follower, I try to approach each issue by asking, "How do I understand Jesus' actions and words concerning this?"

I can live *shalom* with God whether or not the rest of the world receives or rejects it.

But I can't make you have *shalom* with me. We can't make them have *shalom* with us.

We mustn't make believe that Christianity is merely Jesus and me living in our happy relationship, whether or not the rest of the world burns. That is decidedly not the Christianity of the Bible. That is not how Jesus describes the Kingdom of God.

And, having said that, I still must remember that following Jesus begins with discovering my own peace with God. If I root everything about my relationship with God in our work for justice in the world, though this is central to God's Kingdom, I make external activity substitute for embracing God's spirit in my own soul.

So I need both to find my way back into the *shalom* that God my *shalom*-maker and *shalom*-giver has for me and to grieve the *shalom* we have lost as a people. Only as I am rooted in God's peace within me can I help us seek peace and pursue it together. Only as I recognize the fracturing of our *shalom* as a community does God convict me of the part I've played in this and lead me to repent and grow deeper in unity with the Spirit.

Lord Jesus, help us to work toward peace and justice and reconciliation and love. We mourn how far we are from these. We grieve where our nation has claimed these but committed their opposite. Restore our shalom, *with you, within ourselves, and make us agents of change. Make us instruments of your peace. In your name, Jesus. Amen.*

16 Kindness Is More

"In a world where you can be anything, be kind."

One job of preachers is to point out when all of us are nodding and smiling but not actually applying things to our lives.

Honestly, I think many of us read this and think, "Yeah, *they* should be more kind."

Grammatically, of course, this exhortation does not address "them." The subject of the sentence is "you understood" (thank you, Mr. Knox). So it would read,

"In a world where you can be anything, [you] be kind."

It's talking to us. Reminding us. Exhorting *us*.

What does it want us to do?

First, let's distinguish between "nice" and "kind." I'm not a big fan of "nice." "Nice" generally strikes me as superficial, whereas it's difficult to be superficially kind. I'm not certain kindness even works at a superficial level.

"Nice" tends to be about how we want others to perceive us, whereas "kind" requires a commitment to care about the other person. Grace is kind but we don't tend to associate it with being nice. When I speak harshly to someone and, instead of snapping back in turn, they ask, "Are you okay?"–which I'm not–I would not label that as "nice." They show me grace by being kind, by caring about how I am and why I am behaving this way, rather than retaliating.

Kind is paying enough attention to see what someone might need from us, even if they don't ask. Kindness is doing good to people to whom no one else pays attention, to people who might even make us look bad if we associate with them. Nice doesn't do that. Nice might say "Hi" to the person holding the sign asking for help, but nice doesn't stop and enter a conversation, make eye contact, ask for a name and remember it. Kind does that.

In a world where you can be anything, be someone who stops to talk with a person holding a sign asking for help.

"But Mike—"

Yes, I know. So many objections. Some of them reasonable and well-argued. But that's what I'm telling you, kindness doesn't make those arguments. Kindness doesn't dig a trench to fight over why I shouldn't help someone. Kindness spends its energy helping. Kindness sees with different eyes.

We can't be kind in the abstract or from a distance to people with whom we have no connection. If I feel bad that Syrian refugees are suffering, that doesn't make me kind. I might imagine that it does. I might take that as part of my picture that I hold up for myself and say, "Oh, Mike, look how kind you are! You feel bad for people." (Or "badly," if I want to imagine myself both grammatical and kind.)

Again, I'm not looking to quibble on this. It's a good thing to feel bad(ly) when we see others suffer, and sure as heck better than feeling indifference, superiority, or that insidious belief that somehow they're getting what they deserve and I, here not suffering, am also getting what I deserve. Yeah, that one is grotesque. I'm not naysaying a soft heart. I'm just discussing how being kind is reflected, always, in action, in choice, in volition. "By their fruit, you will know them." Matthew 7:20. By our fruit will we know ourselves, if we're honest and more committed to our character and growth than to our appearance. I hope we are.

In a world where you can be anything, be someone who looks for opportunity to affirm others, who looks for strengths to call out, not weaknesses to exploit or mock. Look for good in people *that they can't see* and call their attention to it. Again, kindness thinks about the other, not just self. In a world where you can be anything, encourage, affirm, appreciate, empower. Don't flatter, compliment. Don't be creepy about it. Don't get offended if they don't take it the way you want them to. Kindness understands that, in this moment, it's about them. Kindness means we care more about the person we're affirming than how we look affirming them. If you affirm something about which they feel sensitive, a sore spot or an area in which they've been criticized or feel insecure, they may not know how to take it. They may try to fend off the affirmation, argue, or dismiss it.

"Well screw you, I was *trying* to be nice!"

Guess what. Kindness doesn't say that. Nice does. I mean, probably it says it nicer, at least aloud. "Well, I beg your pardon and bless your heart." You know, acceptable, G-rated put downs. Because nice wants to *look* nice and be recognized for it. Kind knows that some of the most impactful affirmations get some of the worst initial responses. Kind understands that wounded people don't always trust motives, don't always believe a compliment or take it at face value. Sometimes wounded people just *can't*. I don't know how many times I've said something I hoped would encourage and the other person turned it around to be a put down.[11] (Full disclosure, I'm a bit of a master at this, myself). Sometimes that means clarifying; other times, we just need to let the seeds grow and look for further opportunities. When you tell someone who feels stupid that they are smart, you set off some serious dissonance. This is good, because that ugly thought needs to go, but now there's an internal battle roiling as the negative voices attack the intruder, the kind word. And, by association, maybe you.

"But Mike," someone objects," this is *complicated*. I just wanted to…"

Be nice. I know. That's what nice says. I've said it. Absorbing someone's lashing out for trying to love them is one of the kindest things you can do. It's not rewarding, certainly not initially.

It is, however, loving. Kindness asks more of us.

I'll offer one more example of "kind." In a world where you can be anything, be the person who takes the side of the bullied. Refusing *to* bully is kind, especially when you feel pressured to join in. So is looking for those who get bullied or abused and letting them know you see them, you hear them, you validate their hurt.

This especially matters when the bully denies wrongdoing or the world seems committed to affirming the bully, which, to an injured person, sounds a whole lot like "What happened to you doesn't really matter. What really matters is *them*!" Standing with the victim becomes even more crucial when

---

11 This is a separate category from "You thought that was an affirmation when you told the stranger/co-worker/waitress 'Hey, Baby, nice hips' and she glared at you." If you don't have that one figured out yet, we should talk privately; you may have some ground to cove before "kind."

the bully plays the victim. This takes many forms. We're seeing a lot of evangelical leaders caught in/confessing abuse recently. I shudder to think how many more haven't been caught or stopped. I seek to be about grace for everyone, but do you wonder what it sounds like to a person who has been abused when the discussions focus solely on "How soon can we get this [abusive] person back into ministry?" What does this sole focus on help for the abuser say to those *still suffering abuse?*

Kind sees that. Kind hears those words as a person trying to survive and recover would hear them. Kind reaches out, speaks up, embraces and offers ears to hear, space to scream, validation. Kind doesn't factor in popularity. Nice might say, "Well, all sin is the same and we all sin" (a theological twisting of Scripture, by the way), but kind says, "What they did to you was evil and you have every right to feel this rage; God doesn't expect you to stuff it down or repent of your emotions from being abused."

Kind *understands that healing is messy.* Nice doesn't want mess. Kind enters in, wearing a raincoat and waders if necessary. Kind is *in,* standing with the one suffering, undeterred by public opinion, undaunted by the mess.

In a world—okay, sorry, I have to do this—in a world *in which* you can be anything: cool or indifferent, self-centered or self-serving, superficial or self-righteous or even nice,

Be kind.

And may God change us, all of us, as we try.

Please, God, hear this reflection as a prayer. Let us repent of any superficial niceness that would lead us to care more for appearance than for love of our neighbor. Change our hearts, grow them like the Grinch's, as we try to be kind. Amen.

17 Monday Grace

This is a strange time in the U.S. and a strange time to be a Christian in the U.S. I can quote Scripture passages whole, with no comments or other references, and be accused of being political by other Christians.

So let's talk about grace. In fact, let's talk about grace for a whole week.

Monday grace is the grittiest grace. Monday grace is "I hate you but I'm choosing grace over my anger."

Monday grace is enemy grace.

Monday grace is grace I choose to have for myself when I despise myself.

Monday grace is not butterflies and hummingbirds, rainbows and playful otters grace.

Monday grace is "But God proves his love for us in that while we still were sinners Christ died for us." (Romans 5:8) On Monday, we understand that sinners=enemies: "For if while we were enemies, we were reconciled to God through the death of his Son…" (Romans 5:10)

Monday grace is when your child has just told you how stupid you are, again, then comes to you for advice…and you offer it gently.

Monday grace is when your spouse hasn't noticed any of the nice things you've been trying to do and you decide to keep doing them.

Monday grace can look a lot like gritting your teeth and toughing it out because God doesn't mystically make everything easy. Monday grace means God gives us strength when we refuse to give up and quit, give up and die.

Job's wife told him, "Are you still trying to maintain your integrity? Curse God and die." (Job 2:9) Job refused, then argued with his "friends," cursed the day he was born, and demanded God accuse him face-to-face. What gave Job strength, with boils on his skin and dead children in the ashes of his house, to keep praying? Screaming at and accusing God *is* prayer. Fighting God is remaining in relationship with God. How did Job find the strength to clench his hands onto God's shirt instead of cursing God and dying? I call that Monday grace.

18 Tuesday Grace

Tuesday grace is the grace of ordinary things.

I recently read, "Sometimes miracles are just good people with kind hearts." That's the epitome of Tuesday grace. Good people with kind hearts are shot through with grace, but of the kind we often fail to recognize as gifts from God.

Just good people? That made me laugh. "*Just?*"

Good people with kind hearts *are* a miracle, always, a tremendous miracle of grace.

Tuesday grace is coffee in the morning without realizing it's an extravagance, not a necessity. Tuesday grace is a hot shower, without noticing that running water is a luxury...and even more so hot water.

Tuesday grace is that your dog loves you more than you deserve every day of your dog's life, because that's how dogs are wired.

Tuesday grace is the grace that most of us live by most of the time without noticing.

When we do notice Tuesday grace, we live better. We've opened our eyes to appreciate and not take for granted this grace that sustains us.

Mercy is deserving but not receiving punishment. The servant in Matthew 18 who owed the master so much money begged for patience, for mercy not to be punished right then. But his master gave him grace instead, *forgiving* the impossible debt.

Grace is deserving something negative but instead being given something positive, deserving the consequence of our sin but instead receiving God's love.

"For the law was given through Moses; grace and truth came through Jesus Christ." (John 1:17) The law is you get what you "deserve;" punishment comes when you break the law. Grace came through Jesus. Grace always comes through Jesus.

Tuesday grace is receiving God's love in a thousand little ways and not even knowing. Tuesday grace is when someone smiles at you.

Breathe in.

Grace.

Breathe out.

Grace.

Tuesday.

19 Wednesday Grace

Wednesday Grace is the grace of new beginnings. Wednesday grace is that even though you have never yet succeeded in making this change, you are trying again. Wednesday grace tells us you can, and you should, because there is hope….

There is still hope.

And there is *still* hope.

Wednesday grace is God forgiving us again. Wednesday grace is how we are like God when we have already forgiven them four hundred and ninety times and they ask a four hundred ninety-first time…and we forgive.

Wednesday grace tells us God is *not* tired of us, *not* sick of forgiving us, not weary with our needing help again.

Wednesday grace is the unbelievable news that "God has removed our sins as far from us as the east is from the west."

Wednesday grace is that this unbelievable news is true. It's truer than what you think about your sin. It's truer than what you think about other people's sin.

Wednesday grace tells us that God smiles when we show up, every time we show up, even when we're beating our chests, even when we can't bear to raise our eyes, and not because God is casual or unconcerned with our sin, but because God knows we have come to the right place with our sin. At last.

Matthew 18:

> But the tax collector, standing far off, would not even look up to heaven, but was beating his breast and saying, 'God, be merciful to me, a sinner!' I tell you, this man went down to his home justified rather than the other…

Wednesday grace.

20 Thursday Grace

Thursday grace is the grace found in sadness and separation and grief. Thursday grace is recovery grace.

When you watch someone you love die and their death ends their suffering and you say, "Yes, of course I'm sad, but it's a mercy," that is Thursday grace.

Thursday grace is the grace God gives us in suffering, grace that redeems our suffering and allows us to find joy even in the lightless pit, even in our grief.

Thursday grace is not raging-at-God Monday grace. Thursday grace is that God gives meaning to suffering by transforming us through it, *even when we have brought that suffering upon ourselves*. That's why Thursday grace is recovery grace.

Thursday grace may be the most miraculous grace of all, at least to our human eyes, because it allows us to be grateful even for our addictions, even for our deepest brokenness. We are grateful not because these are good in themselves, but we come to realize that through them we know Jesus as we never would have without them.

Thursday grace tells us that God never leaves bad things simply to rot in our lives, but always redeems them. *Always*. Thursday grace reminds us God *is* our Redeemer.

> For I am convinced that neither death, nor life, nor angels, nor rulers, nor things present, nor things to come, nor powers, nor height, nor depth, nor anything else in all creation, will be able to separate us from the love of God in Christ Jesus our Lord.
> Romans 8:38-39

This is Thursday grace.

21 Friday Grace

We've arrived at Friday grace. Friday grace is grace for ourselves. Friday grace is that we accept ourselves, even love ourselves, *with* our limitations.

How is that grace? How is that biblical?

I am imperfect. I fail and fall short in *so* many ways. I know Jesus and I have a pretty good idea what love should look like in many contexts. The thing I know I should do I do not do, and the very thing I know I should not do, that I do. Sound familiar from somewhere? (Romans or your life, you pick.)

Here's the crazy thing about God: God is not angry at me for falling short. God is not angry with me even though I know better. God does not condemn me for my failures. There is now no condemnation in Christ. No, I'm not taking that out of context. This is precisely the context. Romans 7 goes into Romans 8, thanks be to God. When we complete Romans 8 we know nothing—*nothing*—can separate us from the love of God, but remember we began at Romans 7 with my massive failure to do what I should do, *even though I know better.*

Friday grace is I don't have to hate myself for being imperfect. Friday grace is that I can learn to love my imperfect self because God loves my imperfect self. Is God still working in me to perfect me? Absolutely. But not in a pissy, putting-up-with-this-for-now, kind of passive-aggressive, withholding-approval-until-you-get-it-right way. And if you don't understand that description I just gave, I'm describing every single one of us who struggles to love ourselves.

God loves me more than I love me, and Friday grace is it's okay to love myself like God loves me, with the same grace that God shows me.

That may not be radical for you, but it really might be, too. "Loving yourself" by demanding more and treating yourself harshly until you produce is not grace, certainly not the grace we want to show others, the grace we say—and believe?—God shows us.

Welcome to Friday grace.

Love your neighbor as yourself. You know the grace you have been called to show your neighbor. ("And who is my neighbor?") That's the grace God offers you. That's the grace God gives you to show yourself. From you, to you. You can forgive yourself because God has forgiven you. You can show yourself grace because Jesus has taken your sin to show you grace.

Friday grace. You can choose.

22 Saturday Grace

Saturday grace is beautiful grace. Saturday grace can take your breath away. Sunsets that make you stop whatever you're doing because, for a moment, taking in their beauty becomes the most important thing. A ranch that takes neglected, abused horses and pairs them with neglected, abused children and somehow both, all, are healed. Saturday grace is the kindness of strangers, especially when we've screwed up. Saturday grace is that there are still kind souls in this world.

I included this series because I was seeing too much evil and ugly in this world and I can't make it go away. I can't pray it away. I could bury my head in the sand or make myself numb, but doing so wouldn't solve anything nor help any of us. I *can* point out where hope remains. I can remind myself why we might hope, in spite of all we see and hear. I can change my focus and look for light instead of darkness. So I decided it was time to talk about grace again.

Mountains and oceans and flowers and birds are grace. Music we love is grace. Dancing can be grace. Practicing your art form and feeling that moment—*that* moment, when it clicks, when you find the elusive "it"—that is grace, a gift from God-Who-Is-Creator who made us co-creators.

Saturday grace is the unmistakeable grace we still see in the world, the grace that anyone with an open heart, regardless of beliefs, must recognize. When we've blown off a friend who, instead of guilt-tripping us, shows us extra understanding and offers their support, this is Saturday grace. We sometimes miss grace because we mistake kindness and generosity for what we have coming to us.

Saturday grace is that moment when we know we didn't have it coming.

Martin Luther wrote, "If you could understand a single grain of wheat, you would die of wonder."

Saturday grace means coming to see the world as full of grace. It means not imagining that this is merely what we deserve—which is the opposite of grace—but grasping that this is how much God loves us and this is the love God wants to show us.

Ephesians 3, *The Message* translation:

> I ask him that with both feet planted firmly on love, you'll be able to take in with all followers of Jesus the extravagant dimensions of Christ's love. Reach out and experience the breadth! Test its length! Plumb the depths! Rise to the heights! Live full lives, full in the fullness of God.

In the end, "grace" is a way to say "God loves you, and God's love in action looks like *this*."

And guess what?
Grace is greater than you think it is.

23 Sunday Grace

Sunday grace is the grace of rest.

I had planned on leaving it at that and concluding with a seven-word reflection.

But there is at least one other thing to be said about rest: not all resting is equally restful. Not all down time is equally restorative. We can "take time off" and end up more tired and emotionally drained than when we began.

Resting, escaping, and numbing are not all the same . (There's also a big difference between "dead" and "mostly dead." I'll address that another time.) I suspect this varies with each person, so I will just describe it for myself. There are times when I am tired and what I need most in the world is exercise. I need for my body to move and my mind to stop spinning. Those are not times for me to "rest" by getting online and checking out the latest political happenings. Other times I need to move in order to reflect and let God speak. Those are not the times to binge on the latest Netflix offering.

To "recreate" is to re-create. That makes "recreation" much more important than mere "down time." How do we re-create ourselves? How do we invite God to re-create us? When we are torn down, when we are dulled down, when we are stomped down, we need re-creation. What re-creates you?

We have to find our own recreation. I love to hike. I love to be in mountains, where I see God, where God speaks to me and reminds me that was made for more than hunching over a computer.

Sunday grace.

By the seventh day, God rested. God did. God had completed the work of creation and God made that day holy with rest.

A day of rest is holy. Rest is grace.

God commands us to rest. Rest is grace.

What allows you to rest? What do you have to turn *off* to rest? Do you know when you need to re-create for deeper rest? Can you discern that difference in your state of "tired?" Sometimes we have to resist the temptation to numb ourselves from all this so that we can recognize which kind of tired we are right now.

Why does God make a specific day holy and say "Come, rest with me?" Do we receive that grace?

There are, of course, health concerns of overwork and burnout and stress, studies that show how choosing not to rest can compromise or sabotage our immune systems. We have science to back up our need for rest. God knows.

Sunday grace opens us to all other grace. Without Sunday grace, without rest, we still believe that we earn our worth, our acceptance, our love.

Rest, and believe in grace.

24 Culture Shock, Grief, and Pandemic

I've experienced the emotional states of severe grief and culture shock in the past. Many of us have experienced one, some both, and some neither. Truthfully, I'd hoped never to go through either one *ever* again.

I feel aspects of each right now.

As always, I offer this to relate, validate, and empathize. If it's not you, it may be someone you love.

Not everyone experiences these states the same way, so I offer them as my experience, not the "normal" or even "average" way one goes through grief or culture shock.

In severe grief, your world stops. Everyone else's goes on, which adds to the out-of-body, dissonant sensation. A reason for living is gone and other people didn't blink. You are suddenly staring down at a chasm between you and those not grieving.

Grief is loss. The brain takes time to comprehend, accept, and incorporate loss. That leaves you shocked all over again, every time the loss slips your mind and then comes back…like a brick upside the head. You don't forget so much as your brain keeps trying to register the world the way it should be, with your loved one still here. That's the world you've known. It's hard enough losing that world–for me, the world with my little boy in it–but having to keep losing it, over and over, just seems cruel and bitterly unfair.

Grief is disorienting. You have to figure out how to live in a world that is wrong, that should *not* be this way. Even the most mundane things stop making sense and become wearisome, burdensome. "Who cares if I do this? He's gone."

People, especially those who have been mercifully spared from being dropped to the bottom of this pit, will struggle to understand how *wrong* the world is now. They know you're sad. They're sad, too, sad for you and sad

81

for the loss. But being sad and having your world ripped from you aren't the same. They think you're both going through the same thing, differing only by degrees—they're sad while you're *really* sad--and since they're not behaving irrationally like you are, you just need to sort that out.

Again, feeling misunderstood and misjudged only intensifies the isolation: People don't get it. You're alone in this wrong world. You're in the Upside Down. They're not.

I will tell you honestly, though the grief I'm recalling happened over twenty years ago, even letting my head get in that space to describe it puts me right back there again. In that sense, it never "goes away." The loss of a child is an amputation, not a wound; you never regrow your arm, you learn to cope without it.

So here we are, in this Strange Land of 2020. We're all grieving the loss of our accustomed world. But we're grieving it differently and we've lost different things. Some of us are grieving the deaths of people we love. Some are grieving loss of livelihood, vocation, financial security, graduation. So many different things. We're stuck. Then, as an added bonus, we have the range of responses to what is happening, and I don't want to wade into this right now, but *Man*, that is disorienting!

You look out the window at a spring day and the flowers are blooming, but inside you the world isn't *right*. How can you even put words to that? But it takes a toll. You have to keep going, so you do, but... But. It's incomplete. Something is missing. And the loss keeps coming back, even after you think you've adapted to this new (but not right) "normal."

When our son Isaac died, the grief was so disabling for me that I walked in the dark for six months and God disappeared (subjectively, not theologically) for three years. The most loving people didn't try to fix it for me, or explain how I should be sorting it out. The most loving people—most of whom had also lived through terrible loss—simply stuck by me while I writhed and thrashed and kept praying for me that I would come through.

I did come through it. But it was hell and I would not wish it on my worst, most wicked enemies.

Two hundred thousand people in the US have died, so *all* those families are suffering this loss. None of my children or immediate family have died during this pandemic, but even so I'm experiencing certain emotions that compare more closely with that period than anything else in my life–and I would say I'm *seeing others*, even those who have not lost someone close, appear to experience that body-slam-after-a-horrible-fall shock and disorientation.

Culture shock works differently. As with grief, you also don't feel like yourself, but it makes less sense. No one asks, "Why don't you feel like yourself?" after your child dies (unless they're–never mind. Don't get me started.) Often in culture shock, you're functioning at a very low level but don't fully realize or acknowledge it. People look at you and see no visible evidence that something is wrong. I went through a long, miserable stretch of culture shock when we moved to Nicaragua. I knew there was something wrong with me, but damned if I could put a finger on it, make sense of it, *or* shake it off. Even when you know you have culture shock, knowing doesn't solve it or even clearly define it. My friend who moved there with us described it as "I'm stuck and I can't seem to get any traction."

This part feels too familiar right now as I hear people describe their current emotional state. "There's so much I could get done...except I can't get anything done."

In culture shock, your brain is trying to adapt because the world you knew really *is* gone and you have to learn to navigate this new, strange one in which *nothing works right* (i.e. the way you're accustomed to having things work). People suffering culture shock feel exhausted, irritated, confused, and short-tempered. Sound familiar at all? They feel like they *should be getting more done*. Instead, they find themselves pulling inward and seeking familiar comforts (which are suddenly in short supply) or escapes.

One common strand between enduring grief and coming through culture shock is choosing to move forward and live in the world that is, not the world that should be. The person adapting to a new culture must choose to embrace difference, see the positives, and let go of the frustration that comes with experiencing this discord.

In a weird way, we're all suffering a version of culture shock right now and, I would say, it's a particularly unsettling one because everything *mostly* looks and sounds the same! I'm not suffering the headaches I experienced my first year in Nicaragua, due to a combination of squinting, brain-splittting "I don't get this" and good old dehydration. People around us are still speaking a language most of us understand. The driving is the same, though maybe less of it right now, with some people staying home more. The physical spaces and the faces are still the same, though maybe more confined and perhaps on screens instead of live.

BUT.

But. It's not "the way it's supposed to be," certainly not the way it was from February on back.[12] I would posit we're all suffering a bit of (confusing, undiagnosed) culture shock and many of us who have never experienced this before are feeling really angry with…someone. Someone whose fault this is. Someone who caused this. Okay, some of us who *have* experienced culture shock are angry, too, but I'm hoping we have at least an inkling that our anger is caused by something more than just "them"[13]…even if we are angry at them.

Common symptoms of culture shock: depression, weight gain, interpersonal conflict, and discouragement. Falling back into—or even developing new—addictions. Frustration that flares into rage.

Good times, right? Does any of this ring a bell right now?

I have different advice for coming through grief and culture shock, but the overall message boils down to: survive.

Do what you need to do to get through this while causing yourself and those around you as little damage as possible.

In my first year in Nicaragua, my supervisor told me, "A good day is one in which you get up, don't hurt your children, and don't leave." I loved him

---

12 Whether or not that was "the way it's supposed to be" is a different and much longer conversation. The quick answer is "no." But it was what we'd grown accustomed to as "normal."

13 Misdirected anger caused by culture shock is one of the big reasons missionaries don't get along and not getting along with other missionaries is the number one reason missionaries "fail" on the mission field. I'm not even certain anymore if "fail" is the right term for it, but I'll tell you it sure doesn't feel like succeeding

for that. It significantly alleviated the crushing failure I felt, relief I desperately needed in order to keep on breathing and putting one foot in front of the other. I would not have spent seven years in Nicaragua had I not gotten through the first year and I could *only* get through the first year by accepting that the culture shock phase sucks, it's life, and I just had to survive.

This sucks and it's life and you just have to survive.

If you do better than that, awesome! I mean, *awesome!* If you can smell the flowers or plant flowers, teach children or paint (a wall, a painting, your fingernails), write or read or keep going to work that has gotten *so much harder* (or stranger), freaking *hooray for you!* I'm serious. The bar is very low right now. That's how getting through culture shock works. Lower the bar. Be more patient with yourself. I see us coming apart at the seams, turning on one another, growing hostile, looking for someone to blame. This phase, for many of us, sucks.

A good day is one in which you wake up, don't hurt yourself or those you live with, and don't give up. Many things I hear and read every day tempt me to give up. But I'm still having good days; I haven't given up.

You may not be experiencing the pandemic this way. You may be thriving and have no idea what I'm talking about. More power to you and I think you should look around and see whom you can help.

I am doing okay. As I said, I can see elements of both heavy grief and culture shock in myself and, perhaps, even more in others. I say "perhaps" because I'm interpreting what I see and of course I could be wrong. A friend suggested that some people's apparently irrational behavior during shelter in place is in fact trauma response. That made sense of it for me. I'd started thinking along these lines already and his statement brought the dots together to make a picture.

I offer this to you. If it rings true, I encourage you to consider this lens not only for your own responses but for others', as well. None of this is meant to excuse terrible, self-destructive choices, but if the heaviest thing you're carrying right now is negative self-judgment, I urge you to set that down. Yes, easier said than done, but let yourself try. As I said in my satirical "I Did Better Last Pandemic," attacking yourself for feeling awful isn't going to make you feel less awful, but it can make things worse.

Some people can give themselves grace and others of us need to be convinced. God offers us grace all the time. We may not be so generous to ourselves. But you know what? People in grief, folks in culture shock, they deserve a break.

Including if that's you.

Jesus, we see little of the world and none of it objectively. Our perspective is so limited, even of ourselves. Often we can't tell when we're messed up, so we attack ourselves and feel bad about feeling bad or get down on ourselves for being down. Help us to receive grace for ourselves when we cannot meet our own expectations, and when we just can't, period. Walk with us through this difficult time. Give us compassion for ourselves and empathy for others as we make it through each day and choose not to give up.

25 Believing the Best, Optimism, and Wishful Thinking

Come, let us reason together.

Believing the best of someone is perceiving them as accurately as you can while choosing to focus on their positive qualities, affirming their character, and trying to encourage and draw forth the good you can see. You can believe the best of someone who appears horrible, who has done genuinely despicable things. That's how prison ministry works. In fact, that's how grace works. If God won't see the potential for good, for redemption, in people inclined to self-destructive, sinful behavior, we're all doomed.

But we're not all doomed. God sees us as we are and knows we have more capacity for good than we realize. That's the Gospel.[14] That's the Prodigal Son. God knows that we have warped the image of Jesus and God *still sees how beautiful and loving we can be.* When we believe the best of one another, we affirm what God sees, that the drug addict stuck in his habit can recover and Johnny Cash can play a concert at Folsom Prison because he understands the darkness they live in. He lived there, too. But he knows they could be redeemed because he was, too. "Each of us is more than the worst thing we've ever done," says Bryan Stevenson. Believing the best in you means that your darkness is not the last word. God's love is.

Optimism is a different animal. Believing the best is central to the Gospel, not denial nor superficial acceptance but clear-eyed hope for choosing good over evil. Optimism is a cousin of hope but can also dwell in the land of

---

14 Some people would be quick to say, "No, the Gospel is that we are totally depraved and have no good in us but God saves us anyway." In my view, we are created in God's image and God *never* stopped loving us or seeing that image in us, even when we warp and twist it. God made us in love and made us to be like Jesus. God still sees that capacity in each of us and God's spirit works in us to bring that out. That's how we are transformed into the image of Jesus.

make believe. I'm an optimist. I *choose* to be a hopeful person, often directly in the face of my depression and a constant barrage of negative thoughts. But optimism is not identical to biblical hope. Biblical hope is rooted in God's faithfulness and the certainty that all *shall* be well, even if nothing appears well in my limited range of vision. Biblical hope declares that we'll be okay, not because God will prevent bad things from happening but because in Jesus, we can endure bad things, including death. Biblical hope is perhaps the most powerful force on earth, stronger even than greed.

Optimism is simply hoping for the best, but optimism is *not* always rooted in the hope that Jesus Christ has resurrected from the dead and overcome every enemy, including death. Sometimes we're optimistic just "cuz we hope good things will happen." In general, I'd rather choose to be an optimist than a pessimist, even though pessimists have sound logic for their position: "Never get your hopes up and you'll never be disappointed." I've decided there are worse things in the world than disappointment. Cynicism, for example.

But we had a baby die in our arms. Optimism says that bad things won't happen to us, because...they won't. Because it's us. "Things work out." Then bad things happen and optimism looks a lot like believing in unicorns. Nice, but an illusion. That was never real. When you thought "things will just work out" but instead things shatter in a way that can never be fixed,[15] optimism tastes like sulfur. If it's joined to our theology, the backlash will injure us. "But I thought God *loved* me!"

We went to a funeral in Nicaragua with one of our dear friends, Carlos, who was burying his little girl. We'd suffered the same with Isaac, so I could talk with him about it, share our experience, and let him know how I have seen God's faithfulness in tragedy. But here's the truth: *most* people in developing countries (and everyone living in poverty) suffer these life-rending tragedies. I mean *much* more often. Their children die young more often. Their mothers die in childbirth more often. Optimism says that won't happen to *us*, but optimism is also the luxury of people who can afford to

_____

15 There is a massive difference between God fixing and God redeeming. Redemption means God brings good out of bad, but losing a child is like an amputation. Amputations aren't "fixed."

make things go our way most of the time. Again, hope in Jesus Christ is that God loves me and Isaac's death does not change or disprove that. I reached that point, but it took me years. You can see how different that is than optimism, the blissful denial that bad things would ever happen to me. Or you. Or Carlos.

I'm perpetually optimistic that I will arrive on time...and I rarely do. A friend dubbed this "temporal optimism" and I thought that a brilliant term. I somehow can believe, in the face of so many years of evidence, that *this* time I'm gonna walk right out of the house when I need to, hop on my bike or in my car, and arrive 5 minutes early. It took Kim years (and years) to convince me that travel time took actual *time, counted on a clock*. "You have to add that time," she'd tell me. Doesn't seem like a complicated mathematical reality, but I resisted, due to my temporal optimism. I'm a little better now–and I mean if you have a *very* fine-tuned instrument you can detect my improvement. Like a clock that counts milliseconds.

But you can see how this kind of optimism doesn't reside in faith in Jesus Christ or hope in God's grace. It's just "I want things to go well so I'm going to believe they will." Sometimes that serves us really well. Norman Vincent Peale made a fortune selling books about *"The Power of Positive Thinking."* "If you believe it, you can achieve it," that sort of thing. I'm not against that on principle, and certainly if you believe you *can't*, you have proven yourself right without ever trying.

But what is the term for a woman's thought pattern who convinces herself that her abusive boyfriend won't hit her again? Is that "optimism?" Or is that wishful thinking? To be clear, it's always a much more complex tangle of thoughts that involves suffering trauma, negative self-image, believing she somehow deserves her abuse, and the ongoing manipulation that he's the only one who could care for her/provide for her/keep her safe (ironically). But in the core of this mental issue we see a repeated insistence that, against all evidence, "he's sorry and he'll never do it again." I consider that a version of wishful thinking. Damaged wishful thinking, a thought process that needs healing as part of the whole healing process. It's wanting to see what isn't there and convincing myself I do.

Wishful thinking, in my view, can become the opposite of clear-eyed believing the best. Believing the best, as I described it, means I will take every necessary step to keep you from abusing me again. If you can demonstrate that you are changing, I may take the chance to trust you again, or I may encourage you and pray for you but not enter back in (I can believe in someone's redemption without *having* to put myself at risk to do so). Wishful thinking and biblical hope can look very similar. But wishful thinking is rooted in "this is the reality I want to see, so I'm going to pretend this is the reality I actually see." As such, it can be wildly dangerous. Instead of clear-eyed recognition of another's sins and faults, it might choose to overlook or ignore them. Wishful thinking and denial are first cousins. In fact, "wishful thinking" is the nice term for an addict's thought pattern.

We're living in a world suffering a virus for which none of us yet have antiviral medicine (clinical trials are happening as I type). It's a *pandemic*, crossing all borders and boundaries. As always, it will hurt and kill people in poverty more. It's also more likely to kill people with other physical vulnerabilities. "Underlying conditions," we keep hearing. But I like that term about as much as I like the term "casualties" when we're talking about young men and women dying. If you've spent your life coping with and navigating a congenital heart condition or your adult life coping with severe asthma (as my father did), how unfair is it that now the pandemic we all face is *more* likely to kill you?

Pretty *bleeping* unfair, I'd say.

This is not a time for wishful thinking. There might be a different term for nationwide wishful thinking. If there's not, we might need to coin one. But if ever there were a time to get over the illusion "It can't happen to me," That Time. Is. Now. COVID-19 isn't picky. It can happen to any of us. If we get it, we might survive it. We might not. But nationally, we're still working together to prevent a much, much worse tragedy.

Denying medical science and the suffering and death other countries have already experienced is wishful thinking. Deciding it will be okay because we *want* that to be true is wishful thinking. Yesterday, I read an estimate of how many people would die if we reopened everything and sent our children back to school now. Stop and hear that. Estimating how many of *our* children will die.

90

Listen to me. I've suffered having a child die. I barely survived. I feel fortunate our marriage survived (most don't). Two percent of our total population includes more children than you want to see die (not just "casualties," remember), and some of them will be your children. Not only can it happen to you, it will happen to you if we pretend that we'll be fine when all evidence tells us we won't. This is not the time for wishful thinking.[16] Wanting it to be different doesn't actually change our situation, any more than it changes the situation for the woman still living with her abuser. What happens still happens, he still does what he does, no matter how hard she tells herself he won't anymore. If she doesn't leave, statistically speaking, he will kill her.

We don't know enough about this virus yet. That's a big part of our problem. We don't (yet) have the capacity to test everyone. We're still learning how immunity works with this virus. We *know* that people can carry it for weeks asymptomatically.

Come, let us reason together. People, many, many people, are suffering in many ways right now *because* we have chosen to shelter in place. I'm *not* saying it's all fine. I don't have wishful thinking about our shelter in place decision. I'm certainly not saying "This is fine and who cares about people's jobs?" I know, I *really* know that domestic abuse–another gruesome euphemism, if you ask me, when we're talking about (mostly) women getting battered by men–is increasing horribly. Likewise child abuse. I know, all too well and far too personally, that depression is hitting us harder because many of our support systems we've worked hard to construct have been removed. Or demolished. Likewise for people recovering from addiction. Our choice to shelter in place comes at a *terrible* cost.

There is also a nightmarish underlying message here that home is so unsafe for so many people. What do we do about that pandemic? Who's developing *that* vaccine?

I don't claim to have any medical expertise whatsoever and I don't have all the information. But I'm representative because, like you, I have available to me the information from epidemiological experts. Like you, I

---

6 Yes, there *is* a time for wishful thinking: Opening Day of the season, when you can still believe your team will win.

also have available to me the information from people who are *not* medical experts who *want* to believe something conflicting with what the epidemiologists are telling us right now. I get that they have motives for what they tell us. But I fear, I truly fear, that decisions upon which the health, the very lives of millions of people (including our children) depend, are being made based on wishful thinking. I pray I'm wrong.

I have heard no one claim "this is all just fine." Those saying we need to continue sheltering in place are not pitting people's lives against our economy, as if these were two opposing options. If we let the pandemic rage uncontrolled, we will see millions of people—no, millions of *us, our* families— die horribly, *and* we will see our economy crash under the weight of it. It's not one or the other.

I keep thinking people get this:
Our only choices are between
  Containing this pandemic as best we can and then recovering from the economic damage
OR
  Refusing to do what's necessary to slow the spread of this virus, watching COVID-19 rage out of control and kill people we love, *and* suffering the overload of our medical establishment and all the accompanying, calamitous consequences to our economy.

I don't know how to weigh increased abuse of women by men in their homes and loss of income versus another one hundred thousand people dying. Yes, we can hope those people wouldn't die if we all go back to how we interacted before the virus spread. That is wishful thinking.

I know this is all scary, even terrifying, and overwhelming. We have to choose not to let our fear drive us to anger against anyone giving us news we don't want to hear. Right now, the fathers of two different young women I've mentored are fighting for their lives, trying to recover from COVID-19. It's getting more personal for us each day. It's easier to indulge in wishful thinking as long as this isn't personal. This is utterly personal.

I'm tempted to excoriate those who have stated that "acceptable losses" or those with "underlying conditions" would be a reasonable tradeoff for us to "get back to business." But I will settle for pointing out that they mean "those people" who will die. Faith in Jesus Christ means we trust that God loves us even beyond the grasp of death while *following* Jesus Christ means we value the lives of those devalued by our society, by our culture, and by those who count their own lives—and comfort—as more valuable. When I'm serious about following Jesus, I remember there *are* no "Those people." Who is my neighbor?

Our people, our families, will die. We're helping save their lives right now. Please, right now, pray for Luis and Scott, these two men who are part of my extended family in Jesus. Then consider how many more we can protect by following our medical experts' recommendations. We need a plan, such as Germany just introduced, to restart everything cautiously, step by step. Support these plans, not the ones that suggest we could have packed our churches on Easter. We were told that the underestimates we received in January, February, and March--when we should have been preparing for the pandemic--were due to "optimism." I agree that it was optimism, as I've defined it here. Or wishful thinking.

Followers of Jesus are called to live by faith. We seek to believe the best of people. This is faithfulness. We should not mistake believing the best for optimism, nor for wishful thinking. Having faith is not wishful thinking *and* wishful thinking is not having faith. We choose to believe in, and hope for, people's redemption, no matter what they've chosen up until now. We do *not* make up our own preferred reality and attribute that to obeying God. Anyone who tries to lead us in that direction is not leading us to walk with Jesus. As people of the truth, we confront people living in *un*reality, as Jesus did, to love them. We do this with humility, knowing how easily we get off track, and within the bounds of trust we've built in the relationship. When we've seen how people behave, making excuses for—or denying—their poor choices is not "believing the best" of them. When we talk about decisions that put lives at risk, this becomes the wishful thinking that gets people killed.

In general, following Jesus does *not* mean always valuing caution over taking risks to be obedient. We're not to protect our own comfort over our neighbors' lives. However, in our current circumstances, erring on the side of caution does fit with following Jesus because *by* erring on the side of caution we protect our neighbors' lives. All our neighbors. If we end the shelter in place too soon, there will be no way to undo this mistake of wishful thinking.

God, get us through this pandemic. Please. Help us to love our neighbor right now, including by doing what we can to protect and keep them safe.

26 Cheery? Civil? Gracious.

Some of us feel happy most of the time and spill that happiness all around.

I'm grateful for those people. I treasure my friends who offer this to the world. My mother-in-law and my mom both live there, so I've been blessed by them throughout my life.

I'm not one. My emotional makeup works a little differently than that.

But I do smile at people and say "Hi" to strangers by choice, not by effervescence. It doesn't bubble out of me; I try to offer it. I'm not faking being cheerful. I'm offering people what they deserve as God's beloved and as my neighbors.

Even smiling is complicated. I'm fifty-one now and some days I don't shave. Okay, many days. Fine, most days. I'm not hideous but I'm not handsome. Smiling at a woman I don't know can come across as suggestive or inappropriate. Women learn men aren't safe because too many men *aren't* safe and we don't wear signs saying "safe" or "unsafe." So I try to smile or greet in a manner the person can feel grace from me.

Sometimes gracious is to cross the street to avoid appearing a threat. Sometimes gracious is a greeting without a smile. Sometimes gracious is asking a question that leads to a life story from someone I just met.

How do we look at people with eyes of grace? Grace is more than civility, even more than cheer. Grace as a greeting is "God, let the moment I pass be a moment of kindness for them. Let this moment of greeting be an encounter with you."

Does God's grace come across in a mere greeting? Does a moment of kindness make a difference? Yes. And yes. Admittedly, often I can't see that difference. But I know because Jesus says it makes a difference. Offering a cup of cold water shows God's love. Speaking a word of encouragement offers healing. I know it makes a difference because Jesus says it makes a difference *in me*.

Loving God, let us walk through the world in grace and *as* grace.

Amen.

27 Lament

What are you grieving?

I've lived through the death of a child and the death of my father. Isaac and Dad died three weeks apart. That doesn't make me an expert on lament, but those experiences of grief have, to a significant degree, shaped my life   I'm not who I was before I lost them, nor will I ever be again. I had to relearn faith in God.

Through public, formal ceremonies like weddings and funerals, we step together from our old reality into the new. Before the wedding day, we all related to these two as single people, but now we together recognize and witness this moment, vow to support their union, and corporately enter into this reality in which the two become one and "what God has joined together..."

When someone dies, that recognition is even more final. After my grandfather died, I missed the funeral. He and I weren't especially close, but he was a good man and I loved him. I had to grieve on my own. I felt out of step with this change, as if no one around me cared—which, save for my wife, was true. People offered me their condolences, but they were not grieving for him. Grandpa meant nothing to my seminary classmates. Memorial services are sad but serve a deeper purpose than we might recognize. We don't avoid sadness if we skip the memorial, we simply miss the step of corporate lament.

When Isaac died, the corporate lament was not enough. My world shattered and everyone else was sad for a while. Six months later, people were ready for me to be over it and start moving on. Not everyone spoke this, but some did, directly or indirectly. I had felt alienated and isolated *before* they started hinting. Or started acting like I was slow getting on with my grief. The best loving my "enemies" I could muster in that situation was to pray they would *never* experience what I had...else they would be forced to grasp from the inside what they could not comprehend from the outside.

In this shared moment in our nation, we are stuck. We *need* to lament. But of course many around us, including folks sitting next to us in our churches, not only refuse to join us in our lament, but they are frustrated (and mocking) that we refuse to join them in their celebration. In some cases, they name our lament—and accompanying resistance—as the one thing holding back the dramatic improvement our country needs. From their perspective, the problem is not what this administration does but our refusal to see it as good.

Imagine grieving your late parent or spouse or (God forbid) child, and realizing at the memorial that some are celebrating. Not celebrating the good of their life, the love they brought into the world, but actively celebrating their death, wearing bright colors, blowing those roll-out paper noisemakers, singing and dancing and laughing because they won't have to see our loved ones ever again.

I think that captures the discord we're in right now.

I have no idea how to solve our difference in experiencing reality. Oh, how I wish I did! Jesus, hear my prayer.

But I do know we need to lament. We've lost so much. We've seen so much horror and suffering committed in our name.[17]

Lament is our appropriate response. Lament for over 210,000 dead from COVID-19 and increasing each day. Lament for division increased, for racism both exacerbated and denied, for misogyny rationalized. We must lament, as Jesus followers, when those in desperate need come to our nation seeking refuge and instead we imprison them. We must lament, as Jesus followers, how these things have been twisted around so that someone could claim they are being done in Jesus' name.

Lament is the acknowledgement of what has taken place among us, whether the death of a baby or the murder of a woman in her bed, that requires we cry out together and step into this new reality. Whether some

---

17 Some will read this and point out we've committed horrors as a nation and that didn't start a mere three or four or five years ago. I completely agree. I'm not trying to write that book. I'm simply trying to encourage us through this time.

among us, even some among our loved ones, refuse to see—or even dance and celebrate when we keen and mourn—we must share this moment of lamentation with one another. I'm exhausted from trying to convince others how bad it is. We know.

We know. So we cry and mourn as a step toward healing and rebuilding all that we've seen torn down. We must lament and cry to God so that we can face this new reality together...and together work toward something better.

God, help us to grieve and lament.

Hear our cry, O Lord. Hear our scream. Hear our wailing and cursing and know these groans of our hearts as the prayers they are. Help us to lament this loss and horror appropriately, healthily, so that we can remember and go forward. In Jesus' name. Amen.

28 Cynicism versus Hope

"All politicians are liars."

"The government will always be corrupt."

"Everybody is just looking out for number one."

I understand the temptation to cynicism. But we have to remember it *is* a temptation, not a wise appraisal of the world.

Cynicism likes to posture as cool. Cynicism tells us that everything sucks and life is bitter and cruel but knowing this and being able to look it in the eye without blinking makes you superior. You aren't one of those saps who gets sucked in by all that Disney unicorns rainbow bull. Some might call you jaded, but you just get it and refuse to sugarcoat anything.

It follows from this philosophy that anyone trying to spread hope or believe things could improve is gullible, foolish, or trying to sell something. Proper response to such lightweights or con artists includes suspicion, derision, and scathing sarcasm.

Personally, I think the whole thing reeks of cowardice. Or, more charitably, it's a self-defense embraced as a worldview.

If I don't think there's any hope in the world, I don't have to try to make things better. I don't have to risk myself to help others. I don't have to risk disappointment. I can turn away when I see refugees dying, when their children starve to death in those pathetic boats before they can reach shore. I don't have to let that rip my heart because it's all pointless and everyone dies and what does it matter, anyway?

Mocking others for remaining hopeful, being willing to risk themselves for a cause, choosing to believe in something, tells me you want to convince yourself that your dark view of reality is true. If you make others' hope look stupid, that proves you're more worldly-wise and intelligent. Hope is for little children…along with the Easter Bunny, Santa Claus, and leprechauns.

Chicken feces.

Being jaded does not make one cool. Being jaded means a person has acquiesced to the spread of evil in the world. That person might not be evil, but is passive in the face of evil; wise people have argued there's not much difference.

I notice that as I get older, the fight to remain hopeful gets harder. I've seen more. I've watched things get worse. I've seen more people die young of cancer, more people kill themselves with drugs and alcohol, more people who were once idealistic movers and shakers hunker down and get comfortable and complacent.

So I'm saying it directly: Cynicism is a temptation and I won't give in.

I believe people can be redeemed.

I believe God changes people's hearts.

I believe forgiveness changes lives.

I believe you are more than the worse thing you've ever done.

I believe that even though things look very dark right now, we're going to turn this tide.

I'm going to continue investing my heart and my life in young people and walking with them through failure and tragedy and chaos because God is faithful and *they* still believe they can make a difference. So do I.

Yes, it appears "safer" to sneer and scorn and refuse to hope. Yes, you can protect your heart from getting broken if you keep it to yourself. Yes, there's too much evidence that politicians lie and the government will remain corrupt and the rich will get richer and people will be selfish and hurt you.

But that kind of safe is a lie, a temptation.

There is no safe investment. To love at all is to be vulnerable. Love anything, and your heart will certainly be wrung and possibly be broken. If you want to make sure of keeping it intact, you must give your heart to no one, not even to an animal. Wrap it carefully round with hobbies and little luxuries; avoid all entanglements; lock it up safe in the casket or coffin of your selfishness. But in that casket – safe, dark, motionless, airless – it will change. It will not be broken; it will become unbreakable, impenetrable, irredeemable. The alternative to tragedy, or at least to the risk of tragedy, is damnation. The only place outside Heaven where you can be perfectly safe from all the dangers and perturbations of love is Hell. –C.S. Lewis, *The Four Loves*

Hope is dangerous, too. I'm going to hope, anyway, not because I'm a fool, not because hoping is the grown-up version of refusing to accept there's no Santa, but because hope is a revolutionary act. Hope takes courage. Remaining hopeful right now, in the midst of all this, is both courageous and faithful. Hope changes us *and* others. When we choose to be cynical, we reinforce that the evil we see cannot be changed. When we choose to hope, we become part of that change.

Hope doesn't mean denying the bad in the world, but looking straight at it and throwing yourself into making things better. Here is my anti-cynicism declaration: The world is such a bad place, it's worth risking failure to try. If we don't have hope, we can't have faith; acting on hope means our faith is active, not mere words or facade.

This is my hope: God's love overcomes hatred and evil...in my heart.

I have much forgiving to do. I believe God can help me to forgive. My hope starts in me and works outward. Is God really going to change people who seem, empirically, committed to greed and selfishness and actual evil?

God can. God has before.

God can change hearts. God can break chains of systemic poverty and generational abuse. God can free people of addiction.

God can change you and me. God can change the world through us.

I hope you believe that.

> He who passively accepts evil is as much involved with it as he who helps to perpetrate it. He who accepts evil without protesting against it is really cooperating with it.[18] Martin Luther King, Jr.

Jesus, give us the courage and faith to hold onto hope. Help us to stand against evil and not accept it, in ourselves or in our country.

----

18 Martin Luther King, Jr., *Stride Toward Freedom*

102

29 Light in the Darkness

This is the darkest time in U.S. politics I've yet lived through. What do I do in response?

I've tried different things. I've gotten angry. I've gotten depressed. I've cussed a lot.

I tried to ignore what's going on. I've immersed myself in the news. I've read the news from varying political positions. I've read international news on what's happening here.

The last three days, I got to help some friends move by driving from Burbank, California back to Wenatchee, Washington. In doing so, I got to spend a ton of time with one of the best people I know. I'm not saying he's one of the best people in the *whole* world, just one of the best people in *my* world. He and my friends who were moving (his son and daughter-in-law) thanked me profusely and repeatedly, as well as feeding me well and putting me up in luxury accommodations. Don't tell them, but I might have paid for two days of getting to hang out with this guy.

As you might imagine, we talked about everything under the sun, though primarily sports, music, and following Jesus. Not in that order.

We talked a lot about grace, his preaching and my writing, and our discussion drove home this one fact: *now* is the time to share more light.

The news is horrible and gets worse every day. Ignoring it feels unfaithful and following it depresses me. I've given serious consideration to developing a new addiction.

"Ooh, Mike, that's dark humor and insensitive to those who deal with addictions."

Yeah, it would be if I were kidding. I decided I have enough challenges without that.

But what people need, always and *especially* now, is hope. Encouragement. Kindness. Reminders that they are loved.

You are loved.

Right now, in this moment, reading this and trying to find—or regain or even remember—your bearings, you are loved. I don't just believe that, I know that with absolute certainty. Not that you will be loved when you make yourself lovable, stop doing bad things you've been doing, or finally start doing the right things. Not when you have the correct views on politics or an accurate understanding of the world. Not when you get people to treat you better, more respectfully, or as you deserve. You are loved right now.

YOU. Are *loved*. Right freaking NOW.

That's the light.

How can I convince you of that? I can't. I don't have that power.

But *I've* realized I plan to do *this* with my one wild and precious life:

God, Jesus who is Christ, the Great and Holy Spirit that holds together and flows through all things, loves you more than you will ever know and more, perhaps, than you will grasp in an eternity with God.

For those keeping score, that's one God, not three (Trinity and all that jazz) who does not have conflicting views on you. God isn't angry with you and taking it out on Jesus while the Spirit tries to win Him over. God isn't biologically male, either, though Jesus was, as a human and God incarnate. But that's just my best understanding and if that throws you or pisses you off, don't let it sidetrack you. The point is, **God loves you**. You don't need a perfect understanding of who or how or why; you *need* to know it's true. You need to know it's real. Being loved and *knowing* you are loved changes us. Maybe not instantly–though sometimes it does–but inexorably, meaning "in a way that is impossible to stop or prevent."

That's pretty cool.

"Yeah, but—"

Stop. Believe me, I have "Yabuts" about God's love, too. Again, I can't convince you. What I can tell you is this: in my fifty-plus years of life it's the one constant I've known. God redeems. God heals. God loves.

You know why that guy I rode with is one of the best people I know? He's been hanging out with God for sixty-some years. He told me he's never felt closer to God or been more excited about God than he does and is right now. He started out as a pastor with a theology that did not focus on God's

104

love. At all. Believing that gave him guilt and shame. Lots of rules. Plus, a clear message that anyone who didn't believe right, meaning *exactly* like his church did, would burn in hell for eternity.

But God's love? Inexorable.

This many years of hanging out with God and my friend exudes God's love. Even when he's making fun of me (not so hard to do), I feel loved. How would you *not* want to spend time with someone like that?

You know what that really means? I spent 1200 miles being reminded that God loves me. Talking baseball and theology and singing along to Bob Seger, Bad Company, and The Doobies and, underlying it all, that constant reminder. God does love me. It was a great way for me to spend three days.

I wish the same for you. Maybe not sitting in a car for twenty-one hours over two days, but to that same depth.

This doesn't magically solve the feces storm we're in right now. I'm not claiming it does nor am I burying my head. It doesn't instantly heal depression or take away our responsibility to fight injustice happening all around us. In fact, it empowers us to oppose injustice.

This is the light we need to remember so we *can* keep going through this darkness. It's the light that reminds us the whole world isn't darkness. In fact, "The light shines in the darkness, and the darkness has not overcome it." (John 1:5)

There are people given over to evil doing evil things and many other people whom I believe have good hearts who are going along with it. I can't explain this and it grieves me to my solar plexus. It discourages the hell out of me. Makes me want to scream. Tempts me to give up on humanity.

But the light shines in the darkness and the darkness *has not, will not*, and *cannot* overcome it.

God's love shines through this evil. God's love shines through my darkness. God, astoundingly, loves those people given over to doing evil. God loves those people who are going along with it.

Most astoundingly to me, God loves *me.*[19]

Therefore, now is the time to shine.

---

19 I'm not being facetious. I know me better than I know them and I know more clearly what is (to me) unlovable in me.

30 Hope

You might be a Jesus follower. You might be spiritual and seeking light in this darkness. You might feel alienated or rejected or even orphaned from your community. Trust me, I know a lot of people who feel as you do. I talk to them every day. I talk with us every day.

I've got two things to tell you, and I'm going to sound irrationally hopeful and confident. I'm here on my couch with our one-eyed dog, Nicki, sleeping on my arm. Maybe a sleeping dog with the lightest of snores—okay, not *the* lightest—makes one feel like everything could turn out alright after all. And I do mean *all*.

Jesus remains faithful. I can't explain why people who pray to the same God as we pray can see things, facts, *faith*, diametrically opposite to how we see them. I've tried and tried to understand and I concluded—maybe five minutes ago—that it's not my job to understand. I can't persuade them. I need to keep speaking the truth that God shows me. I need to show grace and kindness in disagreement. I'm learning to do those.

I'm not debating whether we're in darkness. Part of what makes us feel crazy every day is that somehow we have to debate this fact. That's exhausting. Today's was "human scum," yesterday's might have been "****hole countries," but it's a new one every day. Every day an outrage and every day spin and justification. But we know what's right and this is wrong. Not that we know everything, not that we're perfect nor claim infallible judgment. But this is clearly wrong and we have to speak and act against it. We have to and we are.

You *can* do this. That's the first thing. You can be light in this darkness. You have done it—whether you felt like you were or not—you can do it, and you'll keep doing it.

The worst time in my life came after my father died and, three weeks later, our infant son Isaac died. Darkness closed in on me. Dad died in late

June, Isaac in early July. A moment stands out to me in December when I smiled, maybe even laughed a little, who knows at what, but I was struck by how *strange* it felt, how odd on my face and in my throat. Three years I walked in darkness after their deaths and I didn't know if I'd come out the other side. Yet I did. Each day that I survived and found reason to hope or smile, even found reason to *breathe*, I was moving closer to coming back out into the light. It wasn't all at once. But I did wake up one morning to discover that my sense of God's presence had returned. Theologically, I don't think God showed up again after checking out for three years. But experientially, it was like that.

We *are* moving through this darkness. Today we are closer to being out than we were yesterday. I don't claim to know what coming out of this will look like. But I believe what we're doing each day—finding reasons to smile, seeing subtle beauty in ordinary things, praying any way we can, appreciating what we have even as we grieve all we've lost—is how we survive and how persevering feels. Some days it seems that the only news is bad to worse and then worse again and we've all lost the ability to be shocked anymore (which feels awful in itself). Other days, the dog snoozes on my arm, the polls suggest more people might be grasping our situation for what it is, and I remember more clearly that Jesus has walked with us all through every bad ruler and dark time and while this is new and appalling for us, it isn't new to him.

That's the first thing: **You *can* do this and we *are* doing this**.

Second, how we walk through this darkness matters. We can fight our way through it and do the right things and come out angry and hardened and even hateful. We could fight for the right things and become something other than what we're called to be, what we hope to be. We can fight the darkness and let the darkness in. As I've said before and will keep insisting, in following Jesus the ends *do not* justify the means.

We need one another to keep speaking hope and love and truth and empathy and compassion. No one is beyond redemption. Love transforms. Truth sets us free. Love our neighbors as ourselves. Love our freaking enemies. These aren't clichés or pat answers, they describe the hard and beautiful work of the Gospel. If you've been part of a church and right now those in your church tell you that everything happening under this administration is wonderful and God's plan and the pastor tells you to pray for God's favor for this unfairly persecuted President, look for the people who can understand what you are going through, who can speak truth and life to you where you're at right now. By the same token, if you have a faithful, supportive community right now, whether among your gang of friends or within your part of Christ's body, keep lookout for those who feel cut off and isolated, rejected and adrift. We have to work the lighthouses overtime right now.

Thus, the second thing: ***How* we walk through this darkness matters as much as *that* we walk through this darkness.** We need one another to walk through this with love, with Jesus. We need one another's encouragement and succor (don't get to use that word enough) and refuge. We need to pool our hope and our strength, to lean on another's faith on the days when ours gets shaky. Today mine is strong, undergirded by my dog's snoring; tomorrow might be a different story. I'll check in with you.

Jesus, we are *making it through this. Thank you for your strength and love. Give us hope. Increase our faith. Let love transform us in this darkness. Amen.*

31 Malaise

You might struggle with something and it might be "something everyone does" and you *still* struggle with it. Having people tell us, "Oh, yeah, everyone does that" may be invalidating rather than comforting, because it can minimize or trivialize what we're trying to face.

If you can't seem to get anything done or accomplished right now, that's not unusual but it's still important. That might be depression or the underlying anxiety that comes with We're in a Pandemic and No One Knows How This Will Go. It might feel baffling. *What's wrong with me?*

So you tell someone,

"I can't seem to finish a book right now."

It may be validating to get back,

"Oh, yeah, I can't either."

But it can feel very different to hear,

"Oh, that happens to everyone," or "I never manage to finish books," or "That's not a big deal…"

Now say you're a reader like me or more so. I haven't read nearly enough in the last few months. By that, I mean I have been distracted and frittered away time where I shouldn't (*cough* *social media* *cough*) and have not done good, spiritual reading nor educational reading nor professional development (i.e. novel) reading as I ~~should~~ want to and really enjoy. Instead, I'm in a rut of doomscrolling. Not every moment, but *way* too many moments. If you're a bibliophile and read a book a week and constantly have 4 or 5 books going at any one time,[20] and you realize, "Crap, I haven't read *anything* for three months," that's not just a bummer. That's a

---

[20] There are a million different ways to be a reader, but I've noticed that one easy classification is those who will *not* start the next book until they've finished the current book and those (like me) who have no idea how many books they have going right now. More than one.

symptom.

Your thing might be journaling or fixing cars or hiking or glass-blowing or gardening. It might be your actual job which you like but can feel you're just dialing in right now (yeah, that might be a quarantine joke, and it still might also be true). If you can't do your thing, if you notice you "just don't feel up to it" even though you love it and feel better when you do it, I encourage you to pay attention to that.

If you don't feel like *you*, that's understandable right now.

If you've tried to tell someone,

"I'm not exercising enough" and they respond, "My gosh, you're in such good shape, you should see what *my* scale says!"

or you say,

"I'm not baking like I usually do" and they tell you "Well, you're lucky, because that would just be a bigger temptation right now."

First, I'm sorry that your friend couldn't hear what you were really saying. Second, that's a serious thing for you, even if your barely-functioning level is still the envy of others. Sometimes comparisons are damaging for us not because we're comparing ourselves but because others are comparing and we stop being honest because that isn't fun to hear.

Most people aren't experiencing their "normal life" right now. That *can* be a great thing, as it offers us a moment and a breather to evaluate whether this so-called "normal" is what we still want to choose. But this isn't a step-away vacation. It's a world-wide crisis. So even trying to gain perspective becomes really difficult with the uncertainty and bubbling anxiety.

Added to that, at least in my case, is a constant anger/frustration/discouragement about the current state of politics and especially how people are behaving and treating one another. Turns out, continuous anger for months on end is awful on the body. Who knew? I feel like I'm in a constant wrestling match with myself between lashing out and trying to show grace–trying to figure out *how* to show grace in this context

110

and in these circumstances. If you are going through this, it is depressing you. I don't mean "that's a bummer" depressing, I mean medically-speaking, sustained anger over long periods of time is terrible for our bodies physically and leads to depression.

So don't do that. Don't be so angry.

Ha.

Obviously, it's not that easy. But it *is* that important to address it.

I've written quite a bit about depression because I live with it. If you're prone to depression, of course this is a more difficult time because it's harder to keep our healthy, balanced maintenance routines. You also likely know how to identify your symptoms, so it's more a question of rebuilding these routines with the available pieces.[21] But if you're not used to depression, you may find this disconcerting or even bewildering.

I think many of us are suffering malaise.

Malaise is: "a general feeling of discomfort, illness, or uneasiness whose exact cause is difficult to identify"[22] or "a state in which people feel dissatisfied or unhappy but feel unable to change, usually because they do not know what is wrong."[23]

It's funny, as I picture who might need to hear this, I'm like the guy who has spent his life on crutches explaining how to use them to someone who's never had to deal with a limp before. I can't beat a healthy person with two good legs in a sprint, but I've gotten pretty used to getting around on these and I'm surprisingly agile. If this is your first time having your legs not work and trying to make sense of "crutches first going upstairs or downstairs?" then it really can be a hard learning curve.

Don't beat yourself up for not feeling normal. Feeling bad or off is challenging enough without attacking yourself for it. You can't just take a club to your malaise to get rid of it. Don't feel bad *about* feeling bad.

---

21 I know, that makes it sound easy. "You know, just find replacement activities and structures to rebuild your healthy maintenance routine in our very constrained circumstance that will help just as much as the ones you spent years discovering." Oh, is that all?

22 Dictionary.com

23 *Collins Dictionary*

Pay attention to your symptoms. That means recognize what things *are* symptoms. A wise friend taught me that when my body is trying to tell me something, it's counter-productive to get angry at it for sending the message (*thanks, Rowena*). I don't mean freak out because you had one bad night of sleep. I mean if you've noticed that you have no appetite for the last three months but are drinking more…stop brushing that off. I'm not a tea-totaler. I'm saying pay attention.

Pay attention when others, especially those you love, are telling you what you're not seeing. Some people are hypochondriacs and some are muscle-through-and-tough-it-out. This is for the latter group (the former are already researching their symptoms, believe me). If you know you're off but just choose to ignore it, someone else may be trying to tell you what you won't let your mind or body tell you.

I'm using "malaise" because, if you've never dealt with depression, this sounds much less daunting. I'm using "malaise" here because for many of us right now, everything is wrong and yet nothing is wrong for us personally and it feels like we should be fine, especially because so *many* people have it so. much. worse. Our internal critic might mention there are big, serious crises happening all around us and this is a stupid time to feel sorry for ourselves. But self-care is *not* the same as feeling sorry for ourselves. If someone told you it is, please try to let that go. It may help to frame it like this: if the crises happening right now matter to you, then what do you need to do to take better care of yourself so you can help? Contribute? Do your part?

It's okay if you aren't doing great. Suffering malaise makes sense right now. I think we should probably have enough empathy and compassion that, even if we are personally doing wonderfully, we also feel a bit off, a bit sickened, seeing how many are suffering all around us. Compassion and empathy aren't weakness. We need to cultivate these, not stomp them down.

Since the definition of malaise ends with "whose exact cause is difficult to identify," I'm certainly not going to pretend I have all the answers. I just know how to get around on crutches. I suggest you identify two or three things you can do—not *would* do if you had the strength and felt up to it but *can* do, right now, feeling like this–that you know will lift your spirits. There's a balance between paying attention to why you feel down and choosing what helps to raise you up again.

Pray. Ask God to help you pray if you can't. Pray for help even if only one percent of you believes that God hears and praying might help. God doesn't hold that against us.

BE PATIENT WITH YOURSELF. I can't stress this enough. Feeling this way doesn't mean you're weak. Breathe. Breathe again. Go for a twenty-minute walk (or five, if that's all you can manage) and breathe deeply and mindfully the whole way. Don't expect to snap out of it. The only people who say "snap out of it" don't get how this feels (or, you know, we say it to ourselves even though we'd never say it to someone else). If you can make yourself, cut back on the doomscrolling or whatever your version of overloading on negatives might be. Stop reading the comments on other people's posts or even on your own. Stop arguing in your head with strangers. Stop arguing on social media with acquaintances. Stop spending your precious energy on things that can only drain you and don't help anyone.

Take the time you saved by refraining from that and go do one of those two or three things you identified. If at all possible, *make* yourself do that thing you enjoy (I'm assuming these are safe things to do). This is a fine line, too, being gentle to yourself *and* forcing yourself to do what helps.

Two last things. First, you may realize that you are suffering depression for real. No shame in that. Absolutely none. What we're calling "malaise," when you finally look at it, may be a deeper problem for you with more established roots. That may mean you need to change your habits or even your lifestyle. It may mean you need professional help and/or medication. Hoping it isn't a serious problem won't make it go away. Facing ourselves with honesty takes courage. Doing so is also crucial to loving ourselves, as in "love your neighbor *as yourself*."

Finally, you aren't alone. That might sound clichéd or false. When we get into these negative spirals, whether malaise, depression, or guilt and shame, the biggest and strongest lie is that you're alone, that no one else understands or cares, and therefore you're cut off from the rest of humanity.

I really hate that lie. It *is* a lie. Don't let that lie smother you. I urge you to pray or ask someone to pray for you (or both). Talk to someone who has earned your trust. If you have no one, write me. Seriously. We're not alone in this; we're making it through this together.

You are not alone.

God, thanks that you understand what we're suffering. Thanks that we don't have to convince you or justify why we feel this way. Give us more patience for ourselves. Heal us, Jesus, even when we can't identify exactly what's wrong with us. Restore our souls.

32 Mirth

I have people in my life who struggle between life and death every day. I'm deeply invested in them and I feel their struggle as if it's my own. I'm not overly concerned if those are poor boundaries. A high school friend of mine committed suicide and I had been playing the cool, "I'll-tell-you-if-you-ask" Christian. We'd had many conversations, some of them while he was heavily under the influence, and he knew what I believed, but I didn't want to be one of those pushy Bible-thumpers. I know some people are overbearing and I can be, too (I've been told that at least once). I erred on the side of avoiding that. But my friend's death and my hands-off approach will be one of my life-long regrets. I know God forgives me. I don't imagine that his problems were within my power to fix. I still want a do-over, to let my friend know he wasn't the only one who felt that way, to offer him more hope and grace. Hope and grace have saved my life; they might have saved his.

That's a strange start to a reflection on mirth.

I read that Daniel and Phillip Berrigan, brothers, peace activists and Catholic priests (Phillip was excommunicated for marrying), loved to laugh and celebrate at any excuse. They committed their lives to confronting horrors of injustice, racism, and violence. They immersed themselves in the struggle against a government perpetuating war and deception and a church either supporting or turning a blind eye. I suspect the Berrigans felt as we do now, especially as they saw the Vietnam war dragging on and more young people dying every day. They persevered. And they laughed together.

We laugh because laughter returns us to a state of grace. When our children were babies and we lived in a perpetual state of exhaustion, I would say that one belly laugh from them made all of it not just worthwhile, but a bargain. I used the word "mirth" here, though, because it speaks of joyful, heartening laughter. I've laughed bitterly throughout this crisis, but that laughter does not raise the spirits nor restore grace. It does not heal. It may,

115

however, preserve my sanity and my vocal cords, when the alternative is running through the streets screaming.

But we need mirth. We need joyful laughter, giggling, and forgetful smiles. We need lightness of spirit. The darkness doesn't just threaten to surround us, it threatens to consume us, to saturate us and eat our souls like a cancer. I'm certain I'm not being dramatic here. I'm watching friends who speak up, act, oppose, vote—and they're growing embittered. I won't name names, but I started this book partly for them. I see the same happening to myself. In the words of my favorite band,

> They say that what you mock
> Will surely overtake you
> And you become a monster
> So the monster will not break you[24]

In an earlier reflection we looked at refusing to hate or vilify our enemies. We do that for them and we *most certainly* do that for ourselves. I can't hate my enemies without poisoning myself. There is no non-toxic version of hatred. Some people, victims of domestic violence for example, may need to hate as a defense to help them escape a relationship where they would otherwise be killed. But even in that case, it's a defense that must be released in favor of forgiveness (from a safe distance and over time).

Mirth combats hatred in our souls. Real laughter acts as white blood cells to eradicate the diseased pockets, the tumors that our impotent rage and mounting despair can spread. God designed us this way.

"A cheerful heart is a good medicine, but a downcast spirit dries up the bones." Proverbs 28:23 (NRSV)

"All the days of the oppressed are wretched, but the cheerful heart has a continual feast." Proverbs 15:15 (NIV)

Coming full circle now, I began with suffering others and my friend's death because we have sorrows that we must bear and also bad news in which we can choose to immerse ourselves...but we can drown that way. I think it's a balance each of us must find for ourselves between staying informed and overloading with discouragement. In direct contrast, I must

---

24 U2 "Peace on Earth" again.

seek out joy and mirth and fun. Proactively.

How can I seek mirth? How can I nurture a cheerful heart in the midst of a catastrophe? I don't mean fiddle while Rome burns. I mean celebrate at every excuse and opportunity. I mean look for glimpses of light through the storm.
I mean listen for a baby's belly laugh and soak it up. Let it reach your heart. We need it.

Cheer our hearts, Jesus. Please free us from bitterness and lighten our spirits. Help us laugh joyfully again. In your name. Amen.

33 I Still Believe

This reflection will upset some and encourage others. God may use it to answer someone's prayer or it may motivate some to pray harder for my salvation. I'm not saying these things to be divisive, but to support you if you find yourself questioning your faith due to similar criticism.

I follow Jesus. I believe in grace. I call myself "a Jesus follower."

I haven't left the faith. Those who decided I have, I leave that between them and God (as certainly my faith should be).[25]

Seeking justice, confronting racism in myself and my culture, advocating for women and opposing misogyny and a rape-accepting culture, these are not extra-credit assignments nor extracurricular hobbies for Jesus followers. They are not a distraction from the "real work." They are inseparable from the Gospel. Anyone who has narrowed the Gospel to getting people to say a conversion prayer, even to the extent that they tell you "feeding starving children if no one gets saved is a waste of time" (I didn't make that up), has lost the character of Jesus and, therefore, the Gospel. You cannot separate the Gospel from the character of Jesus, as if salvation were merely a set of objective truth statements to which one must assent.

God is love. The Bible says so. Feeding starving children is love. Ignoring starving children is not love. If you can twist either of these around, you have left the Gospel behind and replaced it with something else. I'm not making that up, just paraphrasing. Jesus said that.

"For I was hungry, and you fed me." "For I was hungry, and you did not feed me." (Matthew 25)

---

25 One of my dearest friends pointed out recently that sarcasm is my second language. I told her I'm certainly more fluent in it than in Spanish. I've tried to eschew most of my sarcasm in this book—yes, that means if you find it terribly sarcastic as is, you can only imagine how it was before I started editing it out. Maybe I should have kept an original version? Just for proof, of course.

If I sound emphatic, I am. I consider this urgent.

I believe Jesus saves us through his love, through his life, through his death and resurrection. I believe God atones for our sins.

If we claim to follow Jesus but live and proclaim values antithetical to his character and teaching, we have have deceived ourselves. The Bible warns that A)This can happen, and B)we're exceptionally adept at self-deception. By "we" I mean "people."

Do not let people shame you for obeying Jesus by showing compassion. Do not let anyone accuse you of betraying the Gospel because they think you love the wrong people. They got angry at Jesus for loving the "wrong" people, too. He didn't back down on that.

I just watched footage of lunch-counter sit-ins. Understand this: those were happening when I was born. This isn't the ancient history of the United States (unless you listen to my youngest, in which case my childhood coincided with the advent of recorded history). I'm not setting up a straw man here: many of the people who violently opposed desegregation also claimed to follow Jesus. When we live the Gospel in the United States, we embrace a *repentance* of our racist past…and present. If we reject that repentance, either by declaring that we are not racist because *we* haven't done this stuff ourselves or by downplaying this history, we choose individualism over seeking God's Kingdom. Moreover, we tell those still suffering racism in the U.S. that it's in their minds, or restricted to this tiny fringe group of blatant, violent white supremacists.

Jesus is weird. He loves people who make the rest of us wildly uncomfortable. He loves us but confronts our desire to settle into a comfortable bubble of friends who reinforce our preferences and biases. If we can't remember the last time Jesus shocked or offended us, um…that should concern us.

Jesus is our salvation; our beliefs are not our salvation. We can make our beliefs into our religion and talk all day about how we're saved, without talking with the One who saves us. It becomes easier and easier to judge others as falling short of our beliefs. We asked forgiveness and received God's love, back when we got saved, therefore we live up to our own beliefs and thus have the right to judge others by the same measure.

But what if Jesus intends to love those people through us, the very ones we're judging? What if–work with me here–Jesus desires to challenge our narrow definition of love by loving *us* through *those* people?

I was told recently that it's not my investment in or love for people that raise concerns, but my mistaken (liberal) beliefs which threaten to lead me astray. Here's the thing: both those beliefs *and* my love for people spring from the Gospel, from encountering Jesus, from having Jesus opening my eyes to his love for everyone. I've always believed this stuff. I'd say I believe it more and understand it better and more broadly now.

I am more, not less, committed to grace. I rely on it more for myself and believe in it more for you. The difference is, now I won't let anyone tell me who shouldn't receive it, nor let them stop me from offering it to everyone. And I know that will make some people angry. But I'm not going to argue with them. I'm going to continue believing in grace for them, too, even as they tell me I've lost my way.

I hope this is freeing for you. I hope you can see that you don't have to answer, much less convince, your accusers. Embracing this may also have a high cost. It may mean that you won't feel comfortable–or even welcome–in a community where you've struggled to fit in. But I've learned we pay a higher cost by being silenced, by constantly wondering if our silence is costing us our integrity, by trying not to upset those who don't want to be reminded about injustice.

Here's another consideration that I failed to account for: while tiptoeing around people's judgment of me, I missed showing love and support to many outside the community. By keeping my voice down so as not to upset, I did not speak up for those outside who were suffering or persecuted. When I frame it this way–my fear of criticism kept me from conveying God's grace to people who experience rejection by the church–I feel kind of sick. And I *definitely* feel done with that.

Little by little, I'm figuring out for whom I'm writing, how this ministry of writing works, how to use my voice and–oh yeah, what *is* my voice? The feedback I get tells me a lot. If you feel like Jesus makes sense to you–love your enemy, love your neighbor, love yourself–but some people's interpretation looks more like hate and exclusion…you aren't alone. I guarantee it. AND this isn't the first time in history, nor in our history. Some Christians defended slavery. Some Christians defended segregation and some did so violently. Some Christians opposed letting women and blacks vote. *While* they did that, some other Jesus followers looked around and said "Wait, this is wrong! I know Jesus, Jesus loves *me*, and I have to work against this to follow him and love others!"

Standing up like that takes courage. We'll get backlash for doing so. Watch Civil Rights Movement footage again. Unjust systems exist because some people benefit from them. Others will also defend them because they don't understand, dislike change, or refuse to see how *they* could be wrong... or how *they* benefit.

We're here now. It's happening. This isn't an abstract discussion or a chapter in our social studies book. I'm discouraged that, as we see many injustices confronted (sometimes by the church, often not), many Christians entrench even further. I'm even more discouraged that so many Jesus followers respond with such hostility and cruelty.

So I'm going to double down as well. I'm going to say this bluntly and maybe lose friends on both sides in the process, though I hope not.

As Jesus followers, we cannot fight injustice with hate and cruelty. We speak truth. We get angry. We stand up. But when we are tempted to retaliate with those same means, then we must pray. God's spirit works in us to love those who hurt us.

Dang, that statement needs a lot of unpacking. First, on my own I don't love anyone who hurts me. On my own, I want to hurt them back. Jesus' spirit in me gives me strength to love instead of hate. Second, "love those who hurt us" does not mean "just keep right on letting them hurt us and call that love." When people hurt us, we confront the sin and we may have to walk away and set strong(er) boundaries to keep them from continuing to sin and hurt us. But walking away can be love while avenging ourselves cannot be. Covering up their abuse is not love; neither is cutting off their hands.

If we follow Jesus--however you might define that—we must root all our actions, our very being *including our resistance*, in love. God loves us and God is love. We are changed by this love. We are changed *when* we love.

I pray we all (still) believe this. *Amen.*

34 Gaslighting

Many things are difficult right now. My constant level of anger, my unusual (nearly unprecedented) difficulty praying, the unkindness, incivility, and full-blown cruelty to which we're all exposed and the constant justification of these.

But I think, for me personally, some other Christians are the hardest to bear right now. That's not fun. I immediately ask "Am *I* the problem?" Yes, I am. At least part of it. I lose my temper, I respond out of insecurity and frustration, I bear grudges. I want to express grace but I keep falling short.

And.

And Christians who gaslight are the rest of the problem.

Okay, that's an exaggeration. But I need to address this because we face it enough that we must take it head on. And let me acknowledge to begin that this can happen and does happen in both directions.

We talk about keeping our faith always above our politics, meaning that our faith must inform our politics rather than our politics inform our faith. I fight for equality and confront racism *because* I follow Jesus. This is where my following Jesus leads my political views. Now I must discern how I can best live this aspect of my faith.

But of course Jesus was not apolitical and neither are we. Jesus confronted the unjust power structures of his time. He spoke and acted against exclusion of those his culture valued least and deemed outcasts. Yes, this was a spiritual issue...*and* a political issue. Jesus leads us to engage secular politics with the values of God's Kingdom. I don't want to convey that we all have the same calling nor that one aspect of *our* calling should become primary for everyone else. God calls us according to the gifts and passions we have and by grace we get to participate in redemption and restoration: ours and the world's.

I'm frequently accused by some Christians of being "political." It's not a compliment. Likewise, I'm accused of being "liberal." Also not flattery. If I oppose the President on moral grounds, *I'm* being political. Whereas someone supporting the President and making this accusation against me implicitly is *not* being political.

Obviously that does not follow logically. But I think the basis of this evident double standard is that many, many evangelicals believe that conservative politics are the default for Christianity. Thus, being "liberal" means *not* being Christian. That's exactly how they mean it. "You are straying from the Word of God and a Christian world view; you are being liberal." Those function as synonyms.

They aren't, of course, and this is a false dichotomy. More thoughtful conservative Christians will acknowledge that neither political party perfectly embodies Christian truth. But in my experience, most still consider conservative political values and biblical values to align more or less completely, though they admit the application of these in a complex and grey world may be less than perfect.

All this, of course, is bizarre under a President who daily embodies characteristics that, were we not discussing political leadership, we would all agree does not resemble Jesus or reflect the fruit of God's Spirit. But here we are.

There's no nice way to say this, so I'll just be direct. Jesus followers— whom I am *convinced* know and love God and seek to love their neighbor— will tell you this President does not do and say things that you have seen him do with your own eyes and heard him say with your own ears.

This is gaslighting.

We know that the current President lies more than normal, more than average, more than other politicians. We *know* this. We read the fact-checking reports. We hear him lie about where his father was born or about not knowing someone...in spite of dozens of published pictures of them together.

But we're told that this is not so. "He tells it like it is," we're told, and "you just don't like it that he's not politically correct."

This is gaslighting.

I have felt crazy during these last four years, in that horribly uncomfortable "Either you're nuts or I am because we can't both be right" way, while friends, not just internet strangers, tell me to my face that I am misunderstanding everything that's happening.

But here's the truth: I'm not misunderstanding. Of course I'm not interpreting everything perfectly nor accurately. But the evidence of our eyes and ears is what it is. If someone tells me—not hypothetically—that by calling out the corruption and abuse of an administration, I am "cheering for our country to fail," then that one accuses me of being a sociopath. That person has declared my criticism of our leaders "unpatriotic." When I object to these accusations—yes, I'm a bit selfish but not generally void of *all* empathy and conscience, as a sociopath is—I'm told that I'm overreacting. I'm a snowflake. I need to take a chill pill. Oh, and I'm suffering from some disorder not found in the *DSM-5*.

People can disagree. Christians can disagree, even over our beliefs. I consider some level of disagreement healthy, because it presses us to continue thinking critically about our views rather than assuming we're right about everything. Complacency and pride are both dangerous conditions for all of us and we name them as dangerous for any Jesus follower. We preach about that.

Likewise, Jesus followers can and even should disagree about politics. None of us hold all the correct positions, much less live them with perfect consistency. We try to take what we understand about loving Jesus and our neighbor, about living God's Kingdom, and apply those to our political context. The application isn't always clear, to put it mildly.

One would wish that we could all acknowledge that we have legitimate disagreements and accordingly treat one another with kindness and grace. Sometimes we do not consider the disagreements "legitimate" and still we seek to love in our confrontation. In fact, that's one purpose of this book: to encourage myself and you to stick with kindness and grace, to remain faithful to Jesus' way to love our family and neighbors *and* enemies.

Another purpose is to validate that being told we're crazy and that we're the problem while the house is, in fact, on fire is gaslighting. More generally, we need to validate for one another that being told we're not Jesus followers for refusing to support an administration that contradicts our fundamental beliefs about following Jesus is both painful and alienating. That position has driven many of us from our home churches and left many others hanging on by our fingernails.

It's given me, and many of us, pause about how even to describe our faith when the former terms have become associated with things our faith requires us to oppose. If, as polls keep claiming, eighty percent of white evangelicals support this administration, we may do our best to show grace in our disagreement and to stand firmly-yet-lovingly for our faith, but a whole lot of people are going to assume we, as Christians or Jesus followers or evangelicals, also support them. I've been told repeatedly, directly and indirectly, that I've lost my way; at the same time, I've been approached by many friends who don't call themselves Christians who want to ask me of "How can you reconcile what you believe with what they're saying?" I'm guessing you had this, too, especially if you've tried to remain in a community of faith that tends to hold conservative political positions and defends what this administration does.

Now would be a difficult time no matter what, trying to get through a pandemic, navigating the civil unrest roiling throughout our country, and seeking to stand against injustice on so many fronts that seem so entrenched. In a world I imagine, these crises would have unified the church, the whole body of Christ, and we would have worked together and partnered with others to stand for racial reconciliation, reform our broken and cruel immigration policy, address our climate crisis, and mitigate the impact of COVID-19, especially on our weakest and most vulnerable. I still dream—and pray—that God's Spirit will unite us in doing these things as part of God's here-and-now Kingdom.

When we have disagreements concerning these things, we can still offer grace and stay in relationship. But when we're told that we've lost our faith, or are suffering a disorder, denying Jesus, or just overreacting and oversensitive, that isn't mutually respectful disagreement. That's gaslighting.

So I'm here to tell you that you haven't lost your way. Name-calling is still wrong. Cruelty is still a sin. Injustice is against God's heart, which is why it's against our hearts; our response to injustice is one example of how we are made in God's image. Following Jesus means the end *doesn't* justify the means. You might be discouraged, but you aren't crazy. I, for one, am grateful for you.

Lord God, these things make me angry. Sorry, Lord, better "I" statements:I get angry when I experience people gaslighting and manipulating and name-calling. I'm terrible at not sinning in my anger. I'm worse at recognizing when I'm being manipulated, so I get even angrier when I finally figure it out. Jesus, I know that other Christians aren't "the rest of the problem," any more than I am the biggest problem. We're all struggling and, to some degree, we're all deceived. But this conflict has grown horrible and we desperately need you to help all of us to see what is true and what isn't. Open our eyes. When we see the truth, help us to hold tightly to it, and to speak that truth in love with compassion and grace. We've been told that we have lost our way for what we believe is following you faithfully. These are not small disagreements. We need you to heal these rifts. Be our Reconciler. Even more, we need you to show us how to be faithful from here. Help us to hear your voice and continue— or repent and change—as you lead us. In Jesus' Name. Amen.

35 Regarding Others In Light of What They've Suffered

> We must learn to regard people less in light of what they do or omit to do, and more in light of what they have suffered.
> --Dietrich Bonhoeffer

I hope to God that God does with me what Bonhoeffer describes. I hope that God evaluates my actions with a view to my sinful brokenness and what's still wrong with me. I hope God views all my malicious thoughts, cruel words, and neglectful, selfish choices with a clear eye that I am the sinful, screwed-up, in-the-process-of-being-redeemed but-still-a-*long*-way-to-go…Beloved. I am God's Beloved. I hope God considers, when I shout at my son Corin later today or punch a wall in frustration or harbor some truly unloving thoughts about our political leadership, not how bad I always am but how much in need of grace I am.

What we have suffered, all of us, is being sinful, broken people in a sinful, broken world. That isn't "an excuse." That's reality. We're all splintered and fractured in so many ways, though some of us hide it better than others.

When the younger son of the wealthy father, the son who "devoured his inheritance with prostitutes," came limping and stumbling on bare, bloody feet, the father had choices:

He could ignore the return of his son. Disown him. Leave him to survive however he might. "You get what you deserve."

He could bring to bear the Jewish Law against this young man now, which the son broke in dishonoring his father. Likely he could have the boy killed. "You get justice with no mercy."

He could listen to the begging apology/admission of guilt that his son had composed and take him up on that entreaty, i.e. take the son on as one of his servants, disinherited and humiliated but not left to starve. "You get mercy but no grace."

Those were all legitimate, legal, *reasonable* responses to the younger son's behavior. Just to review, so we don't gloss over it, the younger son in Jesus' story goes to the father—no background or context provided by Jesus—and demands his share of the inheritance, i.e. what he would get *when his father dies*. He is saying, "Hey, I can't wait until you're dead so let's pretend you're dead now and I'll get my share." You'd be hard-pressed to come up with a more dishonoring, disrespectful statement.

Again with no explanation, the father gives the son what the son demands. The son liquidates his inheritance into cash and leaves. He spends the money wildly, frivolously, impulsively, hedonistically. We can infer that everything he does with his money directly assaults his father's values as a God-honoring Jew. He spends it all. Who knows if he had a plan, but just then the "far off country" where he now lives falls into famine. He goes from wealthy and epicurean to starving and desperate. He finds a job feeding pigs —a mortifying, defiling job for the son of a wealthy Jewish landowner—and still he is starving.

When the young man "comes to himself," an English translation but possibly my favorite line in the story (except for the father's running part), he decides to go back home, though he *knows* it's not his home anymore.

> But when he came to himself he said, 'How many of my father's
> hired hands have bread enough and to spare, but here I am
> dying of hunger! I will get up and go to my father, and I will say
> to him, "Father, I have sinned against heaven and before you; I
> am no longer worthy to be called your son; treat me like one of
> your hired hands."' Luke 15:17-20

I'm guessing you see what I'm building toward. Did the father regard the son in light of what he had done or omitted doing, or in light of what he had suffered?

Grace is a scandal.

"What he suffered?" people will object. "*Everything* he suffered he brought on himself." The young man *deserved* consequences, right? Punishment? What, he's just going to "get away" with all that?

128

Or did he already pay his consequences?

Many years ago now, I embraced the understanding that we are punished not *for* our sins but *by* our sins. It makes all the difference. Does God warn us not to sin because if we do, he will hurt us for it? Or does God warn us not to sin because doing so will hurt us, and God doesn't want us to hurt? Perhaps holiness is not an arbitrary standard but doing the things that make us whole and avoiding the things that shatter us?

Yes, the father could have turned the thumbscrews down much harder. He could have decided that even though his ragged, emaciated son had come through a famine, utter degradation, and failure, he *needed* further punishment. Or justice demanded it.

But the father did *not* make that choice. He embraced and restored his son. He dressed him. He kissed him. He *interrupted* his confession, to call for a celebration!

The father regarded the son in light of grace, in light of what the son had suffered, in light of the consequences he'd already paid for his horrible choices, and in light of his unwavering love for his child. Grace means he gave the boy good instead of the bad the boy had coming. The father didn't just refrain from punishing him—he embraced his son and welcomed him home.

I don't think we can always treat people exactly according to this, as if the father's treatment of the prodigal were a formula. If someone breaks the law, injuring or killing others, we don't simply welcome them home and let them know that they've already paid the consequences of their crime. They haven't yet.

It's also true that we now live in a culture that readily claims victimhood. Having unfair advantages taken away *feels* like oppression. That means when we try to take Bonhoeffer's words to heart, when we follow the model Jesus gives us with the father of the prodigal, we must also discern for ourselves as well as take others at their word. I'm not claiming this is easy or obvious. When I try, it will reveal my own prejudices, as well. But it's a necessary step.

Having said that, here is the difference when we consider others first in the light of what they have suffered: we begin by viewing them with compassion. I have friends who have attacked me, who are attacking my beliefs and ideas. I know we disagree but I don't think that justifies the criticism, name-calling, or questioning of my character. Do I retaliate? Do I cut off relationship? I'm actually quite good at cutting someone down in an argument, though it's a skill I haven't honed in years (and years, praise God). Do I sharpen those swords again? Do I show what a "snowflake" *can* do?

Or can I regard my friends in light of what they've suffered first, before anything else? I have some idea what they've suffered. Not everything, of course. Certainly my first "natural" urge is not to ask "What are you going through that you chose to speak to me this way?" I have to restrain and retrain that first urge. But as another friend pointed out, aren't we *all* speaking out of [our trauma right now, stuck in the middle of this pandemic?

The center of the Gospel may be that God *always* sees me with grace, calling me away from my self-destructive sin but *as God's beloved*, so that I can experience life and share life. The center of the Gospel may be that even when I behave as an enemy, God does not treat me as an enemy. God can see through my evil, through the rags and filth and stench that I've made of the inheritance *I've* squandered, and still see a beloved child in need of redemption. Dying for that redemption—even though I'm bargaining to be made a servant and not restored as a son.

It's complicated. We don't excuse poor behavior, certainly not abuse, even when we understand where it comes from. I'm not suggesting the two choices are attack back or allow horrible treatment. But how different my view when I choose to see my wounded friend who says hurtful things, rather than choosing to see an attacking enemy whom I must defeat.

Truthfully, sometimes the best I can do is remain silent. It feels weak not to retaliate, not to give them "what they have coming." But that silence may break the cycle of attack and counter-attack. Of escalation. Of violence.

The next step, still way beyond my spiritual maturity, will be recognizing that all humanity are my hurting friends who sometimes say hurtful things. I don't mean that people won't hurt us if we just call them "friends." **I mean when we fully commit to loving our enemies, we have no**

enemies. We recognize that they have attempted to make themselves our enemies, but we refuse to cooperate. At that point, we're trusting not merely in our kindness but in God's power to work through our kindness.

As I said, I'm not there. I'm still trying to love my friends who have chosen to treat me as their enemy. But I believe looking through the eyes of the father for his still-beloved prodigal will lead us closer to God. We try to see through these eyes, even if we fail and fail feebly. Even the attempt and failure can draw us closer to God, can help us become a little more like Jesus. If I'm fully committed to loving my friend, I will also speak the truth in love if they are deceiving themselves about their own brokenness/victimhood/martyrdom. When I put it this way, clearly I can't do this for a random stranger who thinks he is getting the short end because he's previously had every advantage and is offended he's not continuing to get them all.

I hope this doesn't sound abstract. It doesn't feel abstract to me. It feels personal and real and hard. But it's life-giving. It offers us an alternative to fight or flight. It offers a different path than defeating our enemies. It certainly offers us a road less traveled. Seeking *shalom* is radical.

If we can even begin to consider the "other" first in terms of their suffering, in terms of the grace we have to offer, then we are growing in grace.

That will be much more satisfying than winning an argument.

Give me your eyes for others, Jesus. Thanks for how you choose to see me. Help me to choose to see others this way, even my friends who have hurt me. I need to grow in grace. I believe you love me and have welcomed me home and you keep welcoming me home. Amen.

36 Help Them As a Priest

When I make my list of Top Ten movies, often I rank *The Mission* near the top. It's not a perfect movie and some of the racial issues sit uncomfortably. It's not a movie I could enjoy watching all the time, as I could *The Princess Bride,* another contender for number one.

But though I've seen *The Princess Bride* ten (or twenty) times more often than *The Mission*, certain lines from *The Mission* stick with me as strong or stronger than *Princess Bride* quotes. That's saying a lot, considering I can lip-synch the entire script of *PB* along with Inigo, Fezzik, and Westley.

I've also come to realize that though *The Mission* excoriates seventeenth century colonialism and the slave trade, its perspective is now dated. I love it for its music, imagery, and especially its powerful depiction of redemption and grace. You should probably stop reading this and go watch it for yourself before continuing.[26] But in case you don't, I'll provide context for my quotes.

Spoiler alert for those of you who have been *meaning* to get around to watching it…since 1986.

Rodrigo Mendoza (Robert DeNiro) is a horrible, brutal man who, among other things, hunted and sold people as slaves and in a jealous rage murdered his own brother. Then, through a process of penance and redemption that is at the heart of the movie, Mendoza leaves behind his life of violence and becomes a priest. Gabriel (Jeremy Irons) is the Jesuit priest who establishes a mission in northeastern Argentina and eastern Paraguay and who helps lead Mendoza to a point at which Mendoza can accept forgiveness.

However, the macro conflict of the movie—and it's at least rooted in

---

26 To be clear, *The Mission* is intense and depicts graphic, tragic violence. With everything else going on, you may prefer to hold off. If you do decide to watch it: does it successfully critique colonialism or reinforce White Savior Complex?

historical events (The Treaty of Madrid in 1750 and Guarani War 1754-56)—comes between the Portuguese government that wants to profit from slave-trading, the powerful leadership in the Catholic church, and these Jesuit priests who have established this mission. Thus, we have this climactic scene near the end of the movie.

Mendoza: I want to renounce my vows of obedience.

Gabriel: Get out.

Mendoza: I want to explain…

Gabriel: Get out, Rodrigo. I won't listen to you.

[pause]

Gabriel: Just you?

Mendoza: No, it's Ralph and John too.

Gabriel: What do you want captain, an honorable death?

Mendoza: They want to live, Father. They say that God has left them, He's deserted them. Has He?

Gabriel: You shouldn't have become a priest.

Mendoza: But I am a priest, and they need me.

Gabriel: Then help them as a priest! If you die with blood on your hands, Rodrigo, you betray everything we've done. You promised your life to God. And God is love!

Some might take this to mean followers of God should not get involved in politics. But Gabriel himself does get "involved" in politics. He confronts the evil and corruption he sees by speaking truth to power. He puts himself between the oppressor and the oppressed.

Gabriel rebukes Mendoza for turning back from his commitment to love—from following and obeying Jesus—and returning to violence-as-solution.

Great art should help us to see ourselves.

So should friends.

My friend Jeremy (not Irons) challenged me whether I spend as much time praying for this President as I do criticizing him and his administration. Yet my friend made it clear that he wasn't rebuking me for my criticisms—in fact he said, "I agree with you about all of it."

I found that fascinating and challenging.

When people tell me I should "pray for the President," usually loud but implied is "You should *shut up* and pray for him." It's more a shaming rebuke than a real exhortation to prayer. They also assume I haven't been praying for him for years. But Jeremy's was a genuine question.

As a result, I prayed more for the current President yesterday than any other day I can remember since this whole [insert your preferred word here] began.

I've been very vocal that we should shelter in place, listen to and support our doctors and nurses, and protect others' lives by helping flatten the curve of COVID-19 cases. We've all seen this go from uncertainty to concern to conflict to hostility. Today, conspiracy theories are circulating that the shelter in place and face masks response is an organized effort to increase government control and/or strip our liberties. I have good friends asking me what is true and what is distortion, clearly because I play a doctor on TV. (I don't really. Sorry.)

"Help them as a priest!"

Okay, I'm a pastor, not a priest, and currently I don't hold an official position or title as "pastor" while I'm doing this writing gig. But I am what and who I am and official roles don't change that. People ask me because I'm their friend *and* their pastor. Jeremy was right; I need to pray for the President more. In this crisis, I need to call us to the way of love, not the way of violence. I'm *not* saying we should stop speaking up about the crisis– political or pandemic–because we *must* speak up; I'm saying we can't answer hatred for hatred, attack for attack. *I* can't. I mean, I easily can, I'm tempted to, but I must not. It's too easy to dismiss, ridicule, and, when people attack me personally, fire back.

At the conclusion of the above scene, Gabriel states:

> If might is right, then love has no place in the world. It may be so, it may be so. But I don't have the strength to live in a world like that, Rodrigo.

I think about this often, too. It reminds me of Paul's quote: "If only for this life we have hope in Christ, we are of all people most to be pitied." (I Corinthians 19:13) I believe in Love, capital-L, not the fuzzy, feel-good,

134

greeting card sentiment that means little—other than for marketing—in the "real world" of dollars and politics and power, but instead the water-in-the-desert, stronger-than-death, worth dying for *and* living for Love of God because God *is* Love (I John 4:8). God loves us and therefore we have the power and the calling to love one another. I know billionaires are getting richer from this pandemic. If people who love money more than other people have this world right and making the most matters most, if might *is* right, then I have believed the wrong stuff and I deserve pity because I've squandered my chips in the only real game.

But I don't believe that. If love has no place in the world, then I don't think it's a world worth living in, anyway. I don't believe we were supposed to teach our children that dog eats dog, kindness is weakness, and that they need to get ready to fight to the death...and add to the ugliness all-too-present in our world. I hope you don't believe that, either.

I'm urging people to stay home and protect themselves and—*more urgently*—our most vulnerable neighbors from COVID-19 not because I'm trying to "bring down the President." I'm praying for him today. His actions and words are bringing him down, not me. I am staying home and doing what *I* can to keep the virus from spreading, to follow Jesus and love my neighbor. I know we're all in crisis here and I am offering what help I can, using the means Jesus taught and modeled.

Jeremy caused me to ask myself, sincerely, have I let myself slip into fighting hate with hate? Have I, like Mendoza, renounced my commitment to Jesus' way of love? The most insidious version of this, of course, is when we take up violence but tell ourselves we're not, or we convince ourselves that we're justified and this is still the way of love.

I recently had a long conversation with a friend who is an ICU nurse. She described how precarious our local situation had been, how close the hospital came to being swamped and overwhelmed by our local COVID-19 cases. I had no idea until she told me. They had to pull personnel from other departments to work in ICU and separate the Intensive Care Unit into two parts: one for COVID-19, the other for everything else. She told me how much money the hospital is losing because so many other departments have been shut down. She also explained how a member of her family is suffering because of the shut down of his small business due to the pandemic. *All* of these things are true.

A close friend is flying today, on the one flight still available, hoping and praying to reach his father's side before his father dies. My friend oversees pharmacies in nine hospitals (he's with the pharmacists, not Big Pharma, to be clear) and has kept me updated from his perspective on how we are faring with the onslaught of COVID-19 cases. At one point he worked forty-two days straight or some such ridiculous number. He told me the news of his father last night. He knows the risks of contagion better than most. He would not be traveling if it were not literally his last chance to see his father alive.

All of these things are true.

"Then help them as a priest!"

Now I'm talking to you, not just me. Jesus followers are the priesthood of believers. (1 Peter 2) We incarnate God's spirit–God's spirit of *Love*–and offer it, offer *ourselves*, to this weary, beaten, brutal world. That's what we do. That is our calling as people in Jesus' image, those who live and bring God's Kingdom here and now.

Help them as a Jesus follower. Help them as the priests we are.

If you're struggling–*of course* you're struggling, not "if"–then let that struggle be part of what you offer, your own empathy, our shared sorrow and grief, and even your anxiety. You don't have to be "strong" or pull it together to help others as a Jesus-follower-priest. Jesus gave himself *in weakness*. So do we. It's one of the things we are most tempted to dodge in this calling.

People are angry. They're scared. Dear friends have let me know I have no idea what I'm talking about and a few have implied, if not stated, that I'm a dupe for a threat that is either not real or horribly, perniciously overblown.

"Help them as a priest."

I'm not screaming back. I'm not attacking. I'm not even defending myself (in case you need evidence of God's existence, this happens to be a miracle). I'm praying. I'm breathing. I'm trying to understand what they're feeling that they respond this way. I *may* be wrong. Clearly I, too, have limited understanding and limited information.

I have tried, throughout this crisis, to urge everyone to take the threat seriously and to protect one another. None of my friends in the medical profession (and I realize, when I stop to count, I have a surprising number of those) has expressed in the slightest that our response to this pandemic is overblown. I have had several express that we're not taking it seriously enough. When I read the epidemiologists' reports and models for the second wave, the threat is far from over.

I hate how much everyone is suffering and that we have a situation in which all of our possible choices *will* cause suffering. I am still convinced that the better we exercise precautions now, the sooner we will come out of it.

"Help them as a priest!"

How *do* I, as a Jesus follower, help you? How do you help me? How do we love, help and, when necessary, carry one another through this crisis?

I don't have all the answers, but I know now I'm asking the right questions.

Thanks, Gabriel.

Thanks, Jeremy.

Jesus, thank you for the many ways you speak to us. Help us to pray for our leaders and remain committed to your way of love, not the way of violence, conquest, or hatred. Please empower us to lead others in your way. We need your spirit of love to move in us so we can offer ourselves, even in our weakness, as you do. Amen.

37 What Matters

It's the middle of the night, 4:30 AM. I know that's close to getting up time for some of you. I've been trying to keep more reasonable hours, go to bed around 1. "Reasonable" for me. That didn't work tonight.

I've been thinking a lot about getting older. It changes your perspective. I realize I've been trying to say a few things in my writing and I keep coming at them from different perspectives, hoping to zero in.

What we do matters. What we say matters. We have a chance to make a difference.

Lin-Manuel Miranda wrote. "I imagine death so much it feels more like a memory." My dad lived 68 years. Rachel Held Evans died at 37. My friend Fred, only 29. And you might think, "Of course you're thinking about death–it's the middle of the night!" But I've been thinking about these things all the time.

Big events are happening now. We're in an election year. People are screaming and arguing that this is the best President we've ever had, the worst President we've ever had, that the fate of the world rides on this election. We're trying to change a racist, sexist culture while some fight back that our attempt at change *is* the problem.

We're in the midst of a worldwide pandemic. We're learning to do life differently, those of us with the resources to protect ourselves and rearrange our lives. Many more can't protect themselves. I'm watching my wife, Kim, relearn how to teach after twenty-plus years. We laughed today that it should make her feel young, trying to figure out how to do this, just like she did when she started.

Everything feels huge right now, oversized, overwhelming. We're enduring too much stress. We're debating over masks. We're debating if the sky is blue, if water is wet, if U2 is great (duh). But it's intractable because somehow both sides believe they have reason on their side, both sides are shouting, "No, *this* is what 'wet' means!"

So I find myself thinking about death a lot, and meaning, and purpose. What of this, if any, would matter to me if I knew I weren't going to be here. "I imagine death so much it feels more like a memory."

I was missing Nicaragua today. It hits me hard some days, catches me off guard, slams me in the ribs. I was driving this afternoon, when suddenly I missed people and that time and place so badly I literally gasped in pain. But our life in Nicaragua wasn't Shangri-La; I wasn't in some perfect state of bliss there. Sometimes I was miserable. I had insomnia for seven years.[27]

So here it is, what I've been trying to say: First, none of this will go as you plan. It isn't under your control. God didn't give you that power to make it work as you see fit. Today Kim left for a meeting expecting she would have one school year and returned knowing she would have a completely different one.

I had so many plans and such determination to make things go a certain way and, for the most part, they haven't. Do I despair? Quit? Try harder? What matters?

Here's my answer:

I will love you in this time that I have. It's getting light now. Day is coming.

I will love in this time that I have. Love is attention and love is encouragement. For those who can, love is fixing plumbing or sewing masks. We express love in a million ways. Love is forgiveness. Love is helping others see they *are* God's beloved, beautiful and worth loving.

Today I heard from a friend who has *had* it–like when Dad shouted "I've *had* it!" Done. Rudeness in exchange for her kindness. Incivility flung at her civility. She concluded that people suck…but she said it a lot stronger. We've all been there. Actually, I'm more concerned about anyone who hasn't been. If you've never gotten overwhelmed trying to love these horrible people–I mean, people, all of us–then either you are the most *shalom*-centered, spirit-filled person I know…or else you're choosing not to love.

It's such a cliché to tell you that we don't have much time so you should love people…but we don't have much time. So love people. Give yourself

---

7 I know, I know, but the difference is, I *can* choose to sleep now.

for the people who can receive love from you. Spend yourself on them.

I feel like we're following Jesus into the darkness, into a world that gets meaner and smaller and harder all the time, that mocks us for offering or expecting anything different. "When someone is polite to you why can't you respond? Why do you give filthy looks or just ignore me altogether?" It becomes *horribly* tempting to do unto others as they've done to us.

I'm overwhelmed and exhausted and so tempted to lash out.

So *bleeping* tempted.

My friend matters. Today. My friends who haven't quit loving and my friends who feel tempted to quit. So I refuse to give in to that temptation. Jesus, give me strength to love and not hate.

No to returning hate for hate.

No to meaner and harder and smaller. No to "Everyone lies so what does it matter?" No to "There is no truth." No to "Kindness is meaningless in a world like this."

"The light shines in the darkness and the darkness has not overcome it." (John 1:5)

Yes to that.

I ache for my time in Nicaragua because I gave my heart there, not perfectly or even adequately at times, but with intention. Heart longing that feels like an elbow slammed in the ribs is a strange reward, but I wouldn't trade it. Yes to giving our hearts.

Here again, in this vastly wealthier place, I don't know how to love well or even adequately, and it's hard here for all different reasons and sometimes I'm miserable, but the light shines in *this* darkness, this "land of plenty with an empty soul."[28] Yes to that light.

Yes to offering what light we can, what light Jesus gives us, in this darkness.

Yes to believing light is coming.

Yes to loving our children, even when they don't like us.

Yes to loving our friends and remembering to tell them we're grateful for them. I'm grateful for you. I hope you know that. Please know that.

Yes to holding out hope that the people in darkness, including those who

---

28 "Offer," Bill Mallonee, *Vigilantes of Love*

seem willfully ignorant and callously cruel, who look to me like the dwarves in *The Last Battle,* choosing darkness and refusing light, will yet have love break through. Yes to praying for them. Yes to offering them light, even still.

I've realized, probably a little slow, that for some I am the enemy. I talk about Jesus and believe in God's love, compassion, and justice. I don't fit their party lines. I insist on seeing a bigger picture. I won't turn a blind eye.

Yes to following Jesus, even against party lines.

Yes to loving those who call me "enemy."

Yes to loving you, friends who give me hope and carry me when I'm hopeless.

Yes to Jesus.

Yes to what matters.

Amen.

Epilogue I: My Thoughts on Kids in Cages

I first published this article in *Relevant* Magazine online on July 12, 2019. It was their "Most Read Long Form Article of the Year." It hit a nerve for many people—I got feedback from friends that it had been shared at more than one embassy in Central America—and moved me on the path that led to this book. It also resulted in my first genuine hate mail, in which total strangers let me know I would go to hell for what I expressed here...another reason I knew many of us needed this book.

I'm including it as epilogue because1)this situation still needs to change and we have to change it, 2)it's my best expression of why *all* of this is neither "just politics" nor "politics as usual" for me, 3)It answers the question "Who are you to say these things?" at least to some degree, and 4)I promised in my sub-title that this book is for "Immigrant supporters." But I left it for last because it's more exhortation (and confession) than encouragement and hits closer to "This is what's wrong" than "How do we respond to what we already know is wrong?"

Why So Many Christians Want To Go On Mission Trips To Help Kids But Don't Want Them Here

Or

My Thoughts on Kids in Cages

A friend just asked a question which got me thinking down some heavy pathways. I'm going to try to get this down before it fades. I'll need to connect some dots, so bear with me.

Living in Nicaragua made me less judgmental. That surprised me. I was extremely judgmental before I moved. I had a set of unrighteous behaviors and choices for which I judged those around me, friends and strangers alike. I knew I had a problem, but so did they have a problem! Look at all that unrighteous behavior!

My heart was ugly. Who knows, maybe I was right about their poor choices, but my anger and superiority were vile. Then I moved to Nicaragua. Then I became a missionary, a Jesus follower willing to leave his comfortable home and life to suffer for the Gospel and live in an impoverished nation without an air conditioner or a dryer. If pride is the root of being judgmental, you might predict I would become unbearable.

Instead, I crashed and burned. I slammed into culture shock, suffered heavy depression, failed in a whole slew of ways, and got way too near the edge for comfort. Instead of becoming more self-righteous, I came face to face with how we are, all of us, a bunch of train wrecks and disasters. No, some of us don't realize it, but we all are. Grace is greater. Grace is greater than our train-wreckedness. Grace is greater than our unrighteous behaviors. Grace is even greater than our unbearable self-righteousness. Thank God.

I didn't do nearly the good I had hoped to do, but I did some. I loved some people, far more feebly than I imagined I would. I didn't change the world. I didn't change the culture. But I learned this: *We want, desperately, to see ourselves as good.* But doing good costs much more than most of us are willing to pay, and being good? Oh, seriously. So we work out a very narrow, very circumscribed standard for our own goodness. This likely has nothing to do with God's view of us. We just need to be acceptable in our own sight.

Jumping tracks now, but not really: Short-term missions. Short-term missions are a perfect example of both an opportunity to know Jesus and an opportunity to feel good about our own goodness. We can sacrifice for two weeks. We can get dirty and suffer inconveniences and image ourselves to be laying down our lives for the Gospel. I know, it sounds like I'm mocking short-term missions. I led eight of them. I believed in them. Because I went on them, my family and I moved to Nicaragua for seven years. I think we did certain things very well on our short trips. We loved some people, we built relationships, we did some good. I regret nothing. I saw lives changed and I saw God do miracles.

And here is the difference between visiting Nicaragua to "do" a mission trip and living in Nicaragua: you can't keep up the image of yourself as good when you live there. It's hard. It's hot, nothing works the way you think it "should," and there are tropical diseases. People drive crazily and risk not just their lives but yours and your children's. Jesus is there, but not in the way you imagined. Jesus isn't there leading you to become a hero. Jesus is there teaching you faith through a poor *costurera* who can't do simple arithmetic but is more generous with her humble talents than you will ever be with yours. Why do we want to go on mission trips to Honduras or El Salvador and help those poor children but we don't want to let those same children fleeing for their lives come into our country?

Here's my answer: letting them come in, live near us, become citizens, and share in our resources requires more than a narrow, circumscribed version of acting good. We feel great about ourselves when we send out Samaritan's Purse boxes. We helped feed hungry kids! But what happens when the hungry kids come to us? What happens when they have no way to support themselves but their parents have chosen to flee here so that they don't starve or get murdered? A box isn't going to do it.

Tell me this: Why does that choice they've made to come offend us? Because we're all so committed to following every law? Seeking asylum is legal in our country. We have a history of desperate people escaping to our

144

country. My ancestors did. Did yours?

I'm a Jesus follower. I have no argument for someone who believes that we should not share our resources with children who would otherwise be raped or burned alive in their homes, because "Why should our tax dollars have to go to them?" When I say "I have no argument" I mean we have no values in common from which I can argue. I can argue basic humanity and minimum requirements of mercy, but so far those have fallen on deaf ears. If the 10 cents or two dollars that would come out of your taxes are more important to you than a starving child's life, and you truly believe this child deserves to sleep on a cement floor in worse conditions that we keep our convicted felons because "her parents broke the law," then I have no hope of convincing you. We understand the world and our responsibilities in it differently.

Assuming you suffer when you see children suffer, I'm trying to speak to you as plainly as I know how: living next to children suffering all the time forces you to find a way to cope. You have to. I went home and ate dinner and fed my children dinner, and I knew some children close by were going hungry.

Yes, I tried to help—I lived there so I could help, I fundraised so I could help, we started a team and started a preschool to help—but they kept on suffering all around me. Do you know why? They're poor. Poverty means suffering. We don't have to see that, most of us, most of the time. I'm going crazy hearing these arguments of "Why should I care? How is that my problem? Why don't they just obey our laws?" while I'm picturing my precious neighbor girls, Ansielli and Daniella, shivering and screaming for their mama in those cells. You and I know those arguments are abhorrent. But we also know, deep down, that we're talking about a lot more now than going on a trip, doing some manual labor, and getting some photo ops with cute children.

We're talking about traumatized children whom our own government has abused—intentionally, knowingly—and no rationalization can make us the good guys. Evil has been committed, in our names, against the very ones of whom Jesus said, "To such as these the Kingdom of God belongs."

I'm not self-righteous. I saw suffering, day after day, and could not solve it, could relieve it only in minuscule ways, and — ready for the honesty bomb?— often had to focus on other things instead of taking it on directly just to be able to continue living there. Very few other missionaries that we knew in Nicaragua lived in the *barrios* with those suffering poverty. We did. Missionary friends told me we had achieved the best balance they had seen of being with the people and still staying rooted in the supportive ex-pat community. We did the best we knew how. And we failed and failed and failed.

I understand why people get excited about a short-term trip but shudder at the thought of wading in with undocumented people. I promise, if you commit yourself to doing something about this cruelty and abuse, you'll be forced to face your own limits. I mean both the limits of your power and the limits of your generosity and goodness. What do you want to give up to offer someone else a better life? Is your comfort worth the chance of alleviating someone's suffering? It may cost you and not work. Up for that?

Now let me tell you what we didn't fail at: giving our hearts and loving people. We didn't raise our neighbors and Nicaraguan family out of poverty—we're still fighting that battle—but we loved them. We made one another family. My recent visit there reminded me. I would not trade any of it, including my depression and insomnia, nor the brutally eye-opening encounter with my own selfish, undersized heart; I would not trade the seven years we gave ourselves in Nicaragua for anything. In many ways, I wish we still lived there.

I'm trying to figure out my part in this immigrant crisis. Of course, there are many crises all over the planet every day and more suffering than we can possibly learn about, much less change. People use that as an excuse to do nothing. Again, I think that's defining our "goodness" in such tiny ways that we succeed in our own eyes, while turning a blind eye to the pain around us. It's so much harder to try and fail than it is to decide it's not your problem and succeed in your own eyes.

I think following Jesus means letting him lead us past our safe and narrow belief in our own goodness. I think we learn our need for grace when we try to love beyond our capacity. I am not saying we sacrifice ourselves. I am saying we look at children in cages and ask God, "What do I do?"

146

Epilogue II: A Few More Thoughts on Life, Death, RHE, and Where I Go from Here

[This one is straight from my blog, unedited, uncensored. I'm including this because it describes my paradigm shift. It might answer questions for you. It might—*I pray*—free you a little, or begin to. At the least, it will fill in more of how I came to write this book.]

Yesterday, I told Kim I'll probably die of optimism.

They'll write on my gravestone "He didn't think he would."

Best laugh I've given her in some time.

I realized on a hike yesterday—only yesterday—that I have found my voice as a writer. It took me a mere twenty years, give or take. Believe me, this was good news. I think I found it before I understood that I had.

But in that same moment, I realized I'm now trying to discern to whom I'm speaking. I think I had confused or conflated those questions. I suspect that's why it's taken me so long: I was trying to answer the wrong question. I thought I was still working out "how?" when really it's "to whom?" The latter is a very different question.

I am astounded, and I hope you are too, at the widespread grieving—and concomitant cry for action—in response to Rachel Held Evans' death. I knew we all loved her, but I had no clue how hard her death would hit me—or millions and millions of others. If you do a quick search (#becauseofRHE) and look at all the personal testimonies about her and the wide range of publications that speak of who she was, you start to get a small sense of what her voice meant to people.

I never met Rachel Held Evans. I'm seeing the photos of friends who got to meet her and in my grief I'm choosing not to feel jealous but something more like awe. This woman loved so many of us f-ed up souls. Go read how many of the testimonies are from the self-identified misfits, the alienated from church, and the seekers for spiritual community. Why do you think people in the LGBTQ community loved her? Why did so many who claimed no faith at all love her blog?

> Ask the women who have careers because of her championing.
> Ask the mothers of gay kids. Ask the queer believers who found welcome. Ask the women who are in ministry now. Ask the ones who found Jesus, who found hope, who found their voice. Literally ask ANYONE from #**BecauseOfRHE**.[29]

Anytime someone dies suddenly and too young, we should stop and ask ourselves, "Am I living well? Is this my true life or a safe, comfortable, anesthetized escape?" Quoting Mary Oliver: "Is *this* what you plan to do with your one wild and precious life?"

When Rachel Held Evans died, I started to grasp the impact of her voice, of the life she lived, how she spoke to us and how that mattered to us. How we were changed by her words. That was a grand use of her one wild, precious, and all-too-brief life. I see Jesus in how Rachel Held Evans lived and loved. I have no higher praise than that.

So here I am. I'm no Rachel Held Evans. Let me just beat you to that, in case you were starting to wonder if you needed to tell me. But I'm listening and I'm watching and I'm paying attention. I swear to you, I'm paying attention. When you're like me (long pause for snide comments) you fight a constant battle against doubt and negative self-talk. I hope no one in your life says to you what I say to me.

But then, in the midst of this slog through the puddle, here comes someone like Kate Lynne Logan, who several life chapters ago was part of my young adult Bible study. Kate Lynne is a singer/songwriter, mom, wife, and queer. She's a superhero. In response to my thoughts on Rachel's death, she wrote:

---

29 From a tweet by Sarah Bessey, which, by the way, comes in the middle of a furious rebuke of *Christianity Today* for publishing someone who should not have been writing about RHE, but that is a different story and Sarah proclaims who RHE was in the face of self-righteous criticism.

I can't stop thinking about her. 37 is just too shockingly young. Her babies. Oh, her babies. Her 3 year old, who will understand that she's gone, and not understand why.

I've followed accounts in the fringe, and she was always a primary voice. I knew who she was and knew what a light she was.

I stopped believing a long time ago. I was once someone who gave her whole life to church and the gospel.

I tweeted that Rachel was one of two Christians who held my respect, of all the hundreds I knew closely and the thousands I "knew of."

You are the 2nd, Mike.

Rachel is deeply affecting me. Her loss is so deep, and I was just a fringe "acknowledge-er."

If there is a god, he's the god who's you're friend. There is no one who could convince me more than people like you and Rachel.

For the record- I know my personal opinion means nothing. It's not like it's some great honor for me to think the things I do. But Rachel was personal.

And you are personal. And when all we know is what's personal….it's all that matters.

So what is the point? (Okay, sorry, crying here. Give me a second. Damn it, Kate Lynne.) For some reason, like a coincidence that isn't, right when I'm wrestling with this question of "to whom," a bunch of people chime in, unsolicited, to tell me how my voice has impacted them. Two examples:

I love how real you are Mike. Unafraid to live and die with the emotion of the moment, and totally unwilling to let that rule you. I hope and pray to continue to learn that balance.

Dude. I love your fiction. I think it's time for you to publish your non-fiction. You have words and truth that the world needs to hear. Seriously!

For a long time, I've believed I can challenge people in the church to think a little more about justice, to embrace Jesus' love and grace for those left out and pushed away. But I don't know if that ever got through.

I know for certain, however, that some people who don't feel loved by Christians have felt loved by me as a Jesus follower. The way I experience God and my own flaws resonates, even though they have nothing to do with church. Some people who can't understand how Christians can follow Trump have come to me to ask "where the hell is God in all this?" (Think I'm joking?) Others who have stuck with church but increasingly feel like outcasts and aliens where they used to be at home compare notes with me and we share back and forth our tiny glimpses of hope.

I have this message of grace and vulnerability and compassion and justice for the poor and oppressed intertwined with "Holy Shit, this whole being a competent adult thing is *hard!*"

That may not be the message for you. That's fine. You may have this competent adult thing wired. Rock on. Stay around for the laughs or go with God.

You may have no interest in a version of following Jesus that questions conservative politics or uses cuss words or suggests that we're *not* entitled to live at the the maximum comfort level we can afford while billions suffer and we decimate the planet which causes those in poverty to suffer even more.

I used to feel bad when people got offended by these things I said and wrote, like somehow I needed to be more compelling or convey my message more clearly or root it more deeply in Scripture.

I'm done feeling bad.

If I'm helping you, that's awesome. I truly hope to. I want you to know that God loves you wildly and that grace is real. I believe with all my being.

But if you're here to argue or to debate why I think Jesus loves gays (he does, madly) or to help me to see the wisdom in trickle-down economics or arming school teachers, well, how do I say this nicely? You are not my audience.

Is that nicer than "I wasn't talking to you?"

Will I dialogue? Absolutely.

Am I suggesting no one should disagree with me? If you think that, this may be the first thing I've written that you've ever read.

But a beloved friend pointed out, not long ago, "Part of what surprises me in your posts is that you seem to think you need to appease the right, as though they are right." Dead on accurate, because I thought that's who I should be speaking to. I keep hoping to be a bridge-builder and peacemaker.

But who am I kidding? I'm a pastor, and will be until the day I die, but I am not being pursued by churches to hire me as their pastor. People know me as someone who pastors them. I'm a "dem fine" preacher.[30] But turn me loose on their organization? Trust me to keep it together and say whatever seems appropriate to *me*? They are not lining up. See above.

I have a transgender son whom I love with all my heart and of whom I'm wildly proud. I believe materialism in the church and syncretizing US cultural values with the Gospel are our besetting sins. I think Trump is a narcissist who displays in his character, day after day, the antithesis of how a Jesus follower should act and speak.

I have known, from the time Jesus showed me he's real and not a fairytale, that I want to spend my energy reaching the people left out, not fighting with the people already in.

Therefore, I'm not kicking anybody out, I'm not disinviting anyone, but I'm saying here that I'm done appeasing and feeling bad and holding back. As I alluded to in my last post, I'm done self-censoring. I no longer believe that doing so is honoring God and I now have a clearer idea what to do with this one wild and precious life of mine. Rachel's death made me stop and reflect. I know my voice and I know my people.

If that all makes sense to you, guess what?

---

30 Can you really get upset at me for using the language C.S. Lewis uses in a children's book? *The Magician's Nephew*

152

Made in the USA
Monee, IL
14 October 2020